D1533892

POWER PRINCIPLES

Courageous Living

HOW I OVERCAME DEPRESSION
& TOOK BACK MY LIFE

COURAGE MOLINA

For information contact :

http://www.couragemolina.com

Interior Layout and Cover Design by: Olivia Heyward

Edited by: Nicole Louise & Kirsten Quick

Cover Photography by: Alicia D. Moss

Power Principles: Courageous Living

The power to change your life lies in 5 key areas: identity, forgiveness, faith, relationships and growth. When you learn how to wield that power and apply the principles it will transform and elevate your life. As you begin to apply the power principles for courageous living you will experience:

- Boost in confidence and improved self-esteem
- Peace in difficult situations
- Strength and courage to step out on faith and believe God for BIG things
- Improvement in relationships and ability to develop and cultivate new relationships
- Motivation and inspiration for both personal and spiritual growth.

Table of Contents

Foreword

As I write this text, I am seated in a relaxing estate in Hollywood Hills with women who I once marveled at from afar. This year alone I've experienced a complimentary 5-star experience in Israel, over ten unexpected speaking engagements, the opportunity to mentor over 50 women around the nation, and a host of other extraordinary memories, milestones, and moments that remind me of who I am. I am blessed to be asked to share this sacred space of text with Courage, who has said yes to her destiny and refused to allow circumstances to define the summary of her story.

What is in the belly of your expectation? Really... sit with that. What is it, in your gut, that you believe possible of your life? I used to think that, if God was in control, He must be a weak leader. Because why would He allow me to be sexually assaulted in college? Where was God when my family was robbed at gunpoint in our own home? Why would He allow me to travel so deeply into alcoholism and depression? Where was He when I needed protection from these circumstances that tried to take me and nearly choked the life out of my story?

I was angry because, coming from the home of an excellent father, I felt His fatherhood was flawed. I thought it was supposed to be according to my needs and on my terms. I thought that He was a puppet that I could string into my world of decisions and doings and He would FIX IT. My waiting on the "fix it man" or my "maintenance God" to swoop in and erase my circumstances almost left me feeling like a victim of His poor parenting with little to no life in the belly of my expectation. My expectation was so low that I reserved no hope for my future, nor belief that I had any access to His grace and mercy.

Sometimes when you get thumped, it knocks the wind out of you. The pile of circumstances that many of us were born into can empty out our expectations and weaken us to the point of desperation. I recall being tired of surviving, not wanting to commit suicide but unclear on how to live. I was hollow on the inside with no courage to breathe new life into my heart and soul. When you surrender to your pain and your circumstances, you take all of the power to transform your world and turn it into a pitiful hole of darkness and confusion. For this very reason, we must remember who God is and what His power is intended to do in our lives. If He sent His son so that we might have abundant life, why would there be controversy over who God is? If we believe that God is love, why do we question His love for us? If we are His great workmanship, why are we unclear on who we are?

What if you could sit with me in Hollywood Hills in this sprawling mansion and look into the sky and believe. Would you believe that your life is meant to be a gift to the world? Would you believe that there is a noble calling on your life, one that will help solve problems for some of the world's most pressing issues? Would you believe that you have the capacity to partner with God and reclaim your story and your dreams?

Would you believe?When you believe, your capacity expands, your imagination thrives, and you meet God with expectation and courage for the day. Like Courage, He has made you bold, brave, brilliant and radiant in your being. Like Courage, He has held you through some of the most challenging times, not to punish you, but to walk you into a higher way of living. Like Courage, He sees you through the lens of love and adoration. What will you do with this knowledge of love? How will you take the abundance of this relationship and shift the lens through which you view life?

I sit here today fully transformed by the power of my acceptance. I receive God's love for me, and that healed my wounds and made me whole. I embrace my imperfections understanding that where I am weak He has made me strong. I forgive myself for the decisions that tore away at my temple, and I have located the treasure within. Consequently, my eyes are set on seeing myself the way God sees me, and loving myself the way God loves me.

As you journey through the pages of this book, see yourself. See your hurts, your pains, your vault of defeats and denials, and look at your setbacks. Press them against the spirit of our loving Father, who is not the weak leader that I confused Him to be. He is so focused on loving you that He's waiting on you to run into His sweet embrace and pour your belief in Him so that you might experience an unfolding of love everlasting like Courage has done in her story. He wants you to be strong and let your heart be courageous so that He can reveal the truth about who you are and His plans for your life. He wants you to see how Courage said "yes" to an ever abounding love that has unleashed a championship fighter who has set the stage for her name to hold true regardless of what the enemy brings her way.

So be delighted in knowing that what God has revealed through His love and His desire for us to experience Him wholeheartedly has brought us to this one moment in time where you get to choose how your story is written and co-create with the master of eternity.

With love and light,

Sybil Clark-Amuti
Co-founder of The Great Girlfriends

Introduction

This is the story of my life. It's my testimony. It's my truth. It isn't a magical strategy that will transform your life in 30 days or less. There's no smoke and mirrors. No gimmicks. What you're holding in your hands, or listening to, is a book about my journey, and some of the pit stops, detours and dead ends that I've come up against along the way. Within these pages, I'm sharing with you the obstacles and challenges that I have overcome in pursuit of living my best life.

One of my greatest hopes is that my transparency will allow you, the reader, to connect with me on a genuine, authentic level. I want you to know, in no uncertain terms, that I am not perfect. I'm not even in the vicinity of perfect, but there is good news, God is not finished with me yet. The people in this book are real. They are people I love and care for deeply. My goal is not to portray anyone in a negative light, but to simply share my truth.

Please be warned. There is some unsavory language in this book. This strong language is not used to be "artistic" or to add shock-value. No. The language is present to preserve history. To change that would be to rewrite history, give you a watered-down version of the truth to make you, or me, more comfortable. Life, for some, can get very uncomfortable, and so it goes with the telling of my story. The language used is limited to conversations, only, and found nowhere else throughout the book.

I pray you don't allow the "language" to keep you from reading and sharing this book. I hope to share my truth with you, and sometimes the truth isn't pleasant or comfortable. I hope you'll stick with me. Understanding how dark my life had gotten, and how deeply pained and distant I was, is a testament to the transforming power of God's love; His willingness to reach down to the deepest depths to rescue and restore. This is my story, my truth, and the principles I have learned along the way. If these principles can change my life, I'm confident they can help you achieve the changes you want to see in yours.

Cultivated in the turmoil of my deliverance is a constant truth that has become my motto: "Courageous living is about exchanging your struggles for strength, and embracing courage as a lifestyle so you can live your best life." I hope you'll stick around to find out just how it all played out...

CHAPTER ONE

My Childhood Was LIT!

My Kin

"Who you some kin to?" That's a question you get asked in small towns when people haven't seen you in a while, or if you look familiar, but they just can't place your face or your family line. The way you answer that question depends on who's asking. You describe who you are related to based on the age of the person asking the question. You pick someone from their age group. If someone older asks me, I say, "Pop's my granddaddy", or "You know my Uncle Charles". Then, you wait to see if it rings a bell. If it doesn't, you continue down the line with the people you are related to until they have a light bulb moment or until they give you permission to stop listing people from your family tree.

MY CHILDHOOD WAS LIT!

I'm Joyce's baby girl. I am technically one of ten, but basically one of four. Let me explain. My mother had four kids, two boys and two girls. Treshawndra, who is 10 years older than me, is the oldest. My brother Marquis, who is 7 years older than me, is next in line. And last, my brother Amario is 7 years younger than I am. I was raised by my mother, so me and my siblings grew up in the same home together. I am also Clarence's daughter, though you couldn't tell it much by our relationship.

Clarence is my biological father, that much I will admit. As the legendary Temptation song goes, "Papa was a rolling stone." He had 7 children. I was the only child between he and my mother. He wasn't really a part of my life growing up; they split when I was about three years old. I have two older sisters and four younger brothers from his side. Although I didn't get to know them all, I found out they are from three different women, two children with each. Shirlrettha, is the youngest of the two girls and the only one I've built a relationship with that extends beyond social media. My brothers Joshua and Samuel, I've seen maybe once, when we were very young. Many years later I saw them again during my senior year in high school. I haven't seen them since. My youngest two brothers are with Clarence's long-time wife. Benjamin was a baby when I last saw him in person, and I've never seen my youngest brother except from a picture I saw on Facebook. I am not even sure of his name.

PLOT TWIST! There is another man I consider to be my dad. I'm Danny's daughter. Technically, Danny is my stepdad. I say "step" for the benefit and clarification of this book. For the remainder of this book I will refer to Danny as my dad. He has helped make me the person I am and he has guided me in my life. I consider his family my own. They remain so to this day even though my parents have been divorced for over twenty years, and by "parents", I mean Joyce and Danny. Clarence was pretty much out of the picture since I was three years old. I never really understood that, but I knew others like me so I didn't feel bad about it.

I grew up in New Smyrna Beach (NSB), Florida, which is a pretty small town. We used to joke about how it wasn't even on the map or, if you drove too fast on the highway you would miss it. It was pretty much segregated when I was a kid. I lived on what they now call the "westside", but when I was little we called it the "black side." This means that there was also a "white side." The town is so small that we were only segregated by our addresses. We all shopped in the same stores, same hospital and restaurants. There were only a few elementary schools, and by the time you reached 6th grade, the kids went to the same middle school and high school, which meant, we were all mixed together, rich, poor, black and white.

We were poor my entire childhood, but that was a well kept secret from me. I didn't realize how poor we were until I was in high school. I never felt poor growing up, and I think that's a good thing. Those experiences can really shape a kid's identity. My mother sewed my clothes, so I always had a nice wardrobe. When it came to shoes, that was a different story. I never had a pair of designer or name brand shoes. When it came to shoes, my mother was very frugal. I didn't realize we weren't getting the "good" shoes because we couldn't afford them, I just chalked it up to her being cheap, which is partially true. When we would go to the store and I would ask for expensive shoes, she would say, "Okay I'll get 'em, and when ya behind get hungry imma tell you to go eat those shoes!"

I was totally oblivious to our socio-economic standing. I never put two-and-two together. When you grow up poor in a neighborhood surrounded by people who look like you, and they don't have designer sneakers either, no one really talks about it. It wasn't something I worried about. Growing up, I didn't know anyone who had a nice house. We all lived in the projects (government housing) and those who didn't weren't much better off. They lived in old wooden houses, nothing to write home about.

Even though I went to school with people who were much better off than my family financially, I didn't hang out with them outside of school. It's not like I went to their houses and thought, "I wish I had a house like this." It never came up. Looking back, I can see that not having my biological father in the picture was nothing out of the ordinary either. To my young mind it was all pretty normal. Most of the homes in my neighborhood were single-parent households. Some of the kids in the neighborhood were even being raised by their grandmothers or aunties. That was the "norm" growing up there just weren't many fathers around.

My Childhood Experiences

My momma did what mommas are supposed to do. She took care of me, taught me right from wrong, made me go to church, encouraged me, loved me and taught me how to have fun. I remember playing games with her as a kid. We played Uno, Checkers and Monopoly. She wasn't one of those mothers that let you win either, she cheated! She was great during the holiday season, still is actually. She loves the tradition and festivities of the holidays, and she passed that love and passion for Christmas down to me.

There were movies we watched every year together: "How the Grinch Stole Christmas," "A Charlie Brown Christmas" and "The Imitation of Life." We drank hot chocolate and eggnog in a house full of Christmas decorations. Whether it was a raggedy wooden house, or a cement block apartment in the projects, it was always a Christmas Wonderland. I LOVE that about my mom. She didn't let our surroundings or circumstances dampen her holiday spirit.

It wasn't all fun though. She made sure I knew we could have fun, but we weren't friends (laughing). I can hear her right now...

"I'm paying the cost to be the boss."
"You cruisin' for a bruisin'."
"I'm the captain of this ship."

I remember thinking, "I wish this ship would sink then!" You know, because the captain goes down with the ship, I know I was wrong for that, but I was just a kid. I had rules, curfews and expectations in school. When I broke any of those, there were consequences. She would make me do chores, which I hated, because I didn't understand why she couldn't clean the bathroom herself. She used it too, didn't she?!

By the time I became a teenager, I wasn't trying to talk to her about anything or hang out with her. I knew if she knew what I was doing, or wanted to be doing, I would never be able to leave the house. But isn't that what momma's are supposed to do?

Even though I was one of four, I didn't really hang out with my sister and my brothers because of the age difference. Remember, my sister is ten years older than me. When I was seven, she was seventeen; she definitely didn't want to hang out with me. When I think about it, I can't really remember any details of how we spent time together. We shared a room and she had two posters, one of Michael Jackson in a yellow sweater, and one of Prince. She also embraced the style of Cyndi Lauper and Madonna. Those were here favorite artists and with us sharing a room, I developed a love for them and their music as well; one that still lives on today. I also remember those hand-clapping games that kids in the neighborhood used to play:

"Miss Mary Mack, Mack, Mack all dressed in
black, black, black, with silver buttons, buttons,
buttons all down her back, back, back...."

I loved those games! She played those with me all the time, and would often come home teaching me a new, more complicated clap pattern to an old rhyme, or a completely new rhyme and hand routine altogether. I thought she was the coolest. My sister was definitely better than yours. When I was in Read-Pattillo elementary school, Treshawndra's drama class came to my school on a field trip to put on a play in our cafeteria. I felt so cool pointing out my older sister to all my friends in class while we waited for the performance to start. Once things were in place, it turned out that the high school kids included the younger kids in the production by picking "volunteers" out of the crowd to play small roles. I remember this day so clearly because of the sheer excitement and pride I had when my big sister picked me to come up on stage to perform in the cafeteria of my elementary school. I assure you still to this day there has never been a more noble and proud tree. When I was eight or nine, she moved out to go to college. About three years later, she returned with my first nephew, Malcolm. He was an adorable baby; I loved him and wanted to be around him all the time. I loved taking him everywhere they would let me, and I was super excited to babysit from time to time.

If you remember, my older brother Marquis, who is seven years older than me, he and I didn't have much of a relationship. This wasn't just because he was so much older than me. It was mainly because we were so different. He was a boy who thoroughly enjoyed doing boy things, while I was a girl who did not! Marquis and his friends would stink up the house, make noise and hang out in his room. He played football and was very popular. So popular, in fact, that he was voted Homecoming King. When you are loved and adored by the masses, your social calendar stays pretty active. He was no exception to this rule. He was obviously in high demand because he rarely made it home by his curfew.

Are you wondering how he managed to stay alive and break curfew so often?

It is hot as Hades in Florida, and central air did NOT exist in the projects. Should have been a crime. Anyway, I slept with my bedroom windows open, and had a box fan on high propped in the window. It felt like central air to me. My brother would spray me through my open window with the water hose to wake me. I would get up, half asleep, and let him in, until one fateful night I didn't. I somehow made it down the short hall, in the dark, and found myself a nice chair to sleep in, which happened to be right next to the front door. Well, my brother was busted, and I no longer had to worry about drowning in bed at night. I guess it was good while it lasted. We still laugh about that to this day!

As a kid I always lived near my cousins, my aunts and my grandparents. So naturally, my cousins were my first and best friends. We were always together. We had sleepovers and were usually the only "guests" at each other's birthday parties or special events. My cousin, Anterrius, and I were together a lot as kids. There are tons of pictures of us as toddlers together, in a wagon, at a parade, the park and even in the bathtub. I was only two years older than him, and I called him my twin cousin because we were so close. Our mommas are sisters, and lived within walking distance of each other our entire childhood. There was even a time we all lived together.

When we were in elementary school, our cousin Duranda, lived in NSB and we spent a tremendous amount of time together. We were inseparable and always wanted to spend the night at the same house. As you can imagine, it could be a bit tricky to get a relative to take all three of us overnight, but we had a system. Just think: who would sign up for three extra mouths to feed, put up with our giggling, shenanigans, and refereeing our disagreements? I can tell you one thing, we did not stay at my house much. You ever heard of a "yes man"? Well, my momma is the complete opposite, she's a "No ma'am". She wore that like a badge of honor. "Momma, can Anterrius and Duranda spend the night?" "No ma'am!"

Good thing for us we were clever enough to have a system. We would start at the top, where we all loved to stay. This was the "golden ticket" of sleep over houses; the creme da la creme. Our very first stop on the: "Can we spend the night at your house? We'll be good!" tour was Auntie Hazel's house. Auntie Hazel is Anterrius' mom, and we adored her and loved staying over at her house. There were so many reasons why, but let me tell you the top three. Auntie Hazel had the best cereal. Please understand that all cereals are not created equal, and to kids, the brighter colors, bigger prizes and most sugar wins! She had Fruit Loops, Sugar Smacks, Count Chocula; the berry version too. One time, she even had Zelda cereal. Zelda! Sometimes, she would have more than one kind at a time, and we could pick whichever one we wanted! Auntie Hazel knew what breakfast was all about, and we loved her for it!

They also had the original Nintendo. Do you remember the huge gray cartridges you had to blow in if the game started to act up? We got lost in those overly pixelated dreamscapes, fighting, racing or collecting coins for hours on end. Another thing that made Auntie Hazel's house so special was she always had these cute little purple velvet pouches, filled with money. It was all loose change, but to a kid it felt like a ton of money. The thing is, it was more than just the money, and all the treats we could buy with the money. I would pretend those cute little purple pouches were from a far away land, and Auntie Hazel was bestowing to us bits and pieces of a secret treasure from somewhere, and one day, when we were old enough, she would unveil the treasure and we'd live "happily ever after" like they do in those Disney movies. There was something magical about those cute little purple pouches as a kid. Now, what wasn't so magical, were the "off times" when she said no. When these rough times challenged us we pulled together and vowed to stay unified in our efforts, to meet our objective: we stay together! With bowed heads and solemn hearts, we would move on to the back up venue on the tour. Remember, the show must go on.

The next stop on our tour was Grandma Caroline. Now, Grandma Caroline is our auntie, but we grew up calling her grandma. She is Duranda's actual grandmother, and who she was living with at the time. We would stay at Grandma's house, but it wasn't as fun as staying at Auntie Hazel's. This venue didn't have much flare and pizzazz. Apparently, Kraft services didn't get the memo about our combined affinity for good cereal, and there was always Chef Boyardee for lunch the next day. I hated Chef Boyardee, still do. Thank goodness I didn't know about "strongly worded letters" back then. I'm pretty sure Grandma Caroline wouldn't have taken any letter of complaint about our collective culinary preferences well, at all. Actually, I'm pretty certain that I wouldn't be alive to write this book if I had mumbled a word.

The acoustics in Grandma Caroline's house were terrible. I managed to always get singled out about how "loud" I was being. I wasn't being loud per se, I just hadn't really embraced my "inside voice" yet, so I may or may not have sounded louder than I actually was. Plus, if she was that easy to wake up, then maybe it was time for her to get up anyway. Clearly, these were just my thoughts, and I would not be alive today if those words ever passed my lips and came out my mouth. I always took my "talking to" with stride, but I remember feeling frustrated to the point that I wondered why I stayed over there in the first place. It always circled back to my cousins. I stayed and got fussed out, and would get fussed out over and over again if that meant that I would get to be with Anterrius and Duranda. Turns out, my love for them proved to be stronger than any momentary discomfort, bland cereal and even nasty ol' Chef Boyardee's red goop and mystery meat. If we were together everything was good, even when it wasn't.

There were times when we tried to sell tickets to the "Can we spend the night at your house?, We'll be good!" Tour and nobody was buying. Desperate times called for desperate measures. We were many things, tenacious being one and when these dark times were upon us, serious decisions had to be considered, sacrifices had to be made and intense strategies had to be executed. Down and completely out of options when nobody said "yes" meant that we'd have to convince someone without children at all to take in all three of us. This wasn't easy, and as a result the venue didn't have all the amenities we desired when we stayed together. Homes without kids our age were a difficult sell.

We ask if we could stay at Pop's house with Uncle Charles. This was "roughing" it. There was no frill cereal, no electronics, no cable, heck, there wasn't even a TV in the living room. It wasn't a complete bust, though, because there was always something we could get into. For one, Pop had a piano, and we were actually allowed to play it. My Uncle Charles had a few harmonicas we could use and even a tamborine. Now that I think about it, we used our imagination more there than at any other house. As I mentioned before, breakfast was a miss, but the snacks and dinner were supreme. We always had our pick of sausage, cheese and cracker gift box sets. The kind with the little strawberry candy with the strawberry liquidy center. We would slice the sausage and use the little mustards and other sauces. For dinner, we usually had some dish with rice or spaghetti, with more sauce than noodles.....This was a WIN! Did I mention the chocolate milk? There was, literally, chocolate milk by the gallon. I didn't understand why they always had chocolate milk in the fridge. It was strange to me, but I didn't question it; simply enjoyed it.

Hanging out with my cousins was the best. We did fun things together, got in trouble together, fought with each other, would also fight for each other, if necessary. When Duranda was about 8, she moved to Germany with her dad who was in the military. We missed her, but there was never a shortage of kids to play with in our neighborhood, so Anterrius and I did have other friends that weren't related to us. After school, once all our homework was done, we would go outside and there was always somebody to play with, chat with, you know do whatever.

I loved the block I lived on. There were ladies who sold frozen cups, candy apples, ice cream, pickles and hot sausages. Back in those days, you didn't need to go to the corner store to get your junk food fix, you could just walk right down the street and get whatever you wanted. All you needed was spare change and you could walk away with an after school snack that fueled your next few hours of play time before the streetlights came on and you had to go home.

The only problem was that I had to go home so early. All the other kids knew it too. I was the first kid to leave the fun outside and head home. I also wasn't allowed to leave the neighborhood like some of the other kids my age most of the them got to ride their bikes to the park up the street, or hang out at the youth center which was a little further away. I was stuck, confined to the limits of my neighborhood and whoever else was quarantined with me while all the other kids were off exploring. In my momma's defense, I was still in elementary school, so maybe leaving the neighborhood wasn't the best idea.

When I was in the second grade, my momma was diagnosed with cancer. I remember being afraid because I thought she was going to die. There was a secretary at my elementary school who I liked a lot. She was kind, funny and gave me candy, so I would just pop in to visit her from time to time. One day, I went to visit her and she wasn't there. She had passed away; she had cancer. When I heard my mother had cancer, I immediately made the connection and thought for sure she would die too.

My dad took care of us while my mother had surgery, and during her recovery. Do you believe that homes have a feel to them? Our home became an empty, colder shell of its former self. It was home, but it was off, not as warm. It's hard to explain. It was home, but at the same time it wasn't. I thought the moment she returned home things would go back to normal, but they didn't, not right away. After surgery, she couldn't really get out of bed, and there was a long tube that came from underneath the covers that lead to a bag filled with a yellow liquid. She was tired, but she was alive, and that was better than the alternative as far as I was concerned. Plus, my dad tried to pick up the slack.

He didn't play games with me or anything, but he did cook. His favorite dish to make was pork chops baked with tomatoes and onions. It wasn't a pretty sight. The pork chops were all white, swimming in the pinkish juices created by the tomatoes. All good cooks know the only way to cook and serve pork chops is to fry them until they are golden brown, and serve them with green beans and mashed potatoes with gravy. DUH! Apparently, dad didn't get the memo because every time he made pork chops, which was a lot, he never once bothered to properly prepare them. Despite his struggles in the kitchen, he did his best to make sure everything ran like clockwork.

Spending more time with my dad meant we were also able to spend more time with my dad's family. Mario, my youngest brother, and I got to spend time with our Grandma Annie Lee, our aunties and our uncles. My dad's sisters were much younger than he was. They seemed more like cousins than aunties. I loved staying with them during the weekend and for days on end in the summer. Those summer days in Cocoa Beach with my grandma and aunts were amazing. Grandma made it her top priority to spoil us rotten. She knew just how to do it too. We could eat whatever we wanted, and we pretty much had full reign over the land; access to ALL the spoils. This was heaven! My grandma transformed her kitchen into a restaurant, ready to take our breakfast, lunch and dinner orders every day during our stay. She would cook pancakes, biscuits, grits, sausage, ham, bacon, and we could eat cereal while we waited on her to finish cooking breakfast. This wasn't the only meal like that, no, it was this way all day, for every meal.

Did I mention the snacks? The glorious and delicious I-don't-have-to-share-any-with-Mario-or-anyone-else-or-ask-for-them-because-they-were-my-own-personal-snack snacks that were available 24-hours a day. Literally! You didn't have to worry about a shortage, either because if you happened to eat an entire box of ice cream sandwiches in two days they would be replenished, post haste. We did, however, have to go to the Kingdom Hall, which was very different from the church experiences I was used to. I wasn't sure what to make of all it; it was so quiet, even the decorations were quiet. No one spoke above what seemed like a whisper. There wasn't anything for me to occupy my mind with, so I often struggled to stay awake.

Everything about it was odd to me, but it was such a small price to pay for all the fun I had while I was visiting my dad's family.

Whenever I think about my childhood, I have to try hard to remember the things that weren't so great. It's like, I learned early on to remember the good, learn from the bad and throw the rest out. My childhood, in my personal opinion, was basically LIT! I was surrounded by family who loved me, parents who took care of me and the best friend cousins in the projects.

CHAPTER TWO

Fighting, Sex, and Dating, Oh My!

Do you remember the show called the *Wonder Years*? It was a show about a boy and his family during his teenage years, mostly told from his point of view. I used to watch that show and I didn't really get the connection between the title and the show, but I liked it enough. As I think about my teenage years, the title of the show makes sense. Wonder Years... I wonder what made me do, say, and think the way I did during my teenage years. As you can see, I had a pretty LIT childhood. How did such a great childhood lead to such a difficult season as a teenager? My poor momma!

I didn't get into drugs or drinking. Well, I did drink a few times, but I wasn't really into it. I did, however, get suspended from school once, maybe twice, okay, a few times. I was suspended from school a few times, and always for fighting. I didn't just all of sudden start fighting as a teenager, no, I was bullied while in elementary school at my bus stop, AND I got my first and last black eye in third grade. I wasn't new to fighting, I just never did it in school. Even as a teenager, I had a love for learning and excelled academically. My education was very important to me, so I avoided confrontation in the classroom at all cost. I didn't have time for that. I was too busy trying to learn. As a result, this was really the best time to say something slick to me, or toss a crazy look my way, because I would ignore it.

My fights took place in the halls, in the cafeteria, walkways and such. I would never have a fight in the classroom. I never wanted to be the reason for distraction or melee. So we're clear, just because I would fight, doesn't mean I initiated or sought opportunities to fight. Fighting was just a natural byproduct of growing up in my neighborhood. It's just how things were. I tried not to fight in school, but sometimes it simply couldn't be avoided. One time, I did get into a fight in PE class. We were outside, so technically that doesn't really count. What was I fighting for? Well, the first time I was suspended it was because a boy said something about my momma. I don't know about you, but where I'm from, it's a perfectly reasonable expectation to get punched in the face after speaking ill of someone's mother. I've always been an overachiever, and like to meet, and often exceed expectations. I was eager to facilitate this kid's desire for pain after he spoke bad about my mother. Like I said before, I didn't look for opportunities to fight, but if one arose, I wasn't one to run. I've never been a bully and I wasn't combative or even difficult to get along with. I just spoke my mind with ease and demanded respect. I was confident, which meant I liked myself, and I wasn't going to allow people to mistreat me in anyway. That was my attitude all throughout middle school.

I was suspended a few times in seventh and eighth grade. The first suspension, in 8th grade, was during the first week of school. Some girl threatened my twin cousin, Anterrius, my A1 since day one, and called him a nigger. I'm not sure what made her say it, and at the time it didn't matter. I just hopped off that bench and was on her like white on rice, without questions, conversations, do not pass go and do not collect $200 dollars. I did not play that crap, not with me and not with my family. Not then and not now, so please don't try it.

My fighting wasn't only contained to school. I was ready in the neighborhood too. Just a reminder, I didn't start anything but if someone else wanted to, I was happy to oblige. I never considered responding to foolishness the same way I did inside the classroom, outside the classroom. It wasn't an option for me back then. I wasn't always fighting though. I had a pretty solid group of friends. Now keep in my mind, when I say solid, what I mean is we were mostly good, and mostly had each other's backs unless we were beefing with each other. You know how that goes. My friend group at the time included: Catisha, Charmaine, Chantel, Tawni and Bridgette. Chantel and I had been friends the longest because we met in the third grade. While time and distance has changed our friendships and how often we reconnect, I still consider all of them my friends.

In our little group there was plenty of personality, sass and confidence. You couldn't tell us we weren't all that and a bag a chips, either. We were willing to fight for each other, and sometimes with each other, or any combination of the two. We were never without some type of drama. Our town was small and it seemed like the older and bigger we got, the smaller and more uneventful our town became. The good thing about a small town is that you can walk to the places you want to go. When we would get bored, we would make rounds to all of our houses, snack, see what was going on, and when we got bored we'd move on to the next person's house. We almost never went to my house; it wasn't really a good hangout spot. Some of our favorite things to do back then were to watch BET, learn all of the latest dance moves and listen to new music. I've always loved to dance and to this day, can listen to anything with a nice dance beat. Like most girls in middle school we were also interested in boys.

That interest in boys, combined with teenage hormones, can be a dangerous combination. Contrary to popular belief, not ALL sexually active teenage girls have low self-esteem or feel pressured by a guy to have sex. I can't recall feeling either. I didn't agonize over my decision to have sex. I never daydreamed or romanticized about it either. It was something that I wanted to do, so I did it. My hormones were in full force and I had no desire to keep them in check. I let them make the decision for me. I was in the seventh grade when I lost my virginity. I had sex with a boy who was just a year older than me.

Let's call him Guy #1. I was friends with his sister, so we were around each other enough. They had moved to our small town that year, or maybe the year before from New York. We were cool. We had no commitment to one another; I wasn't his girlfriend and he wasn't my boyfriend. I didn't think he cared about me in any particularly special way, nor did I hold him in any high regard. He was just a boy. I thought he was cute, I wanted to have sex with him, and he wanted to have sex with me. So, we had sex. When we saw our window of opportunity we took it.

Everyone was doing it. It was what you did in middle school. I knew girls who had sex for the first time in fifth grade. So me being in seventh grade was quite normal, or so I believed at the time. I was supposed to be babysitting my little cousins, but instead of babysitting I was having sex. We were home without adult supervision when it happened. I was allowed to invite a few friends over to hang out and help me babysit. I ended up inviting my friends, plus the cute older boy too. It was a recipe for a hookup.

When all was said and done, I felt bad because I had violated the trust of my cousin and did something that I couldn't undo. I don't think I felt pressured to do it, but once it was over, I definitely felt some type of way about doing it. My momma didn't find out right away, and when she did, I did what any other sane teenager in my position would do. I LIED, duh.

What's crazy is, when most think about kids who have sex at an early age, they think of them as kids who have been exposed to a promiscuous lifestyle in the household or sexual abuse. Maybe they saw their parents with multiple partners, or they didn't have any rules or consequences at home, so they could do whatever they wanted. That wasn't true for me. My mother didn't have multiple partners, she had my dad. They started dating when I was around five years old and they married when I was in 6th grade. I had firm boundaries, curfews and rules growing up. I had to be home before the streetlights came on, even in middle school, which sucked!

I honestly believed, whether it was true or not, that that's what people did. Kids my age, or a little older, were having sex. So when my hormones said that I should be having sex, and I had the opportunity to do it, I did it. That first time wasn't an enjoyable experience. It wasn't horrible, but it wasn't good either. It was actually a bit of a let down. I didn't understand what all the hype was about. The first time was the last time until 9th grade.

"Dating".

Now, in eighth grade I had a friend named Ericka (Hey, girl!). She basically started a dating/matchmaker type of service in middle school. I am not kidding, this was a real thing. The downside of growing up in a small town is, the boys you play with in kindergarten are the same boys in middle and high school. I don't know who said "familiarity breeds contempt," but they were definitely on to something. There was so much history with the neighborhood boys, that it was hard to see them as prospects when it came to dating. To keep it real though, most of them have grown up to be good looking men, with beautiful wives and adorable children ("What's up, fellas?").

My matchmaker friend, Ericka, had gone to school in Daytona for her seventh grade year. Daytona being a larger city than NSB, Ericka had gained access to a larger dating pool than we had back home. She had a bunch of phone numbers of boys from her old school and neighborhood. I have no idea how she got them all, or why she kept them, but I decided that

I wanted some of those numbers. I already decided the boys that I had known for most of my life were not really the boys I was interested in, and Ericka being a great friend, hooked me up with a list of names and numbers of boys that came from Daytona Beach.

Yasss, honey!! This was like striking gold. You have to remember this was before social media, and before cell phones were as common as bubblegum, so it was a big deal for you to call someone you didn't know. I had the courage, naivety or plain old stupidity, to do so. I would call up the prospective guys, most of who were my age or maybe a couple years older, and talk to them. I would basically start dating them if they had a nice telephone voice; this went on into the summer months.

There was a summer program at Bethune-Cookman College, located in Daytona Beach, that my friends and I attended. A bus came to pick us up, there were activities and lunch was provided. I don't remember any of the activities, but by this time, I was much more interested in meeting boys than playing games. Since I knew I was going to be in Daytona each day, whenever I talked to one of the boys from the list I would tell them, "Hey, I'm going to be on your side of town, would you like to meet up?" If they didn't look as good as they sounded on the phone, I would dump them. I only remember one guy being as cute as he sounded, so that relationship lasted the entire summer.

Nothing serious ever happened during those little meet-ups. It was all for my amusement, and it kept me entertained. I guess I might have been hopeful, though. Maybe one of the guys would turn into something more serious, something more real.. whatever that meant.

As the summer came to a close, and I prepared for high school, the desire for a guy to share the same space as me became a little stronger. You know, in high school, everyone knows that you're supposed to date and spend actual time with each other, and all I had was a sweet guy over the phone. It wasn't real enough.

My friend Catisha was hanging out with an older guy, but they were like brother and sister and she was already in a relationship. She and I started hanging out more, which meant I was around her friend too. Let's call him Guy #2. He wasn't like the other neighborhood boys. He was from New York, just like Guy #1. There definitely is a bit of a trend here. Not only was Catisha friends with Guy #2, but I also knew of him because his sister and I were friends in middle school. We shared a common admiration for each other's older brother. She thought my older brother was so fine and I thought her older brother was good looking. So I "knew" him, but I didn't really know him. Anyway, I was super flirty, feeling myself, as they say.

Meanwhile, I hadn't really been using the list because I had started to like a guy named Chris. He seemed nice, sweet and had a great telephone voice. He wasn't from NSB, either. He lived in Daytona. I considered him to be my boyfriend. The only thing wrong was the distance; we never got to kick it in person. Talking to Chris on the phone was great, but it wasn't enough. No matter how much we spoke, it wasn't going anywhere. We weren't progressing. Now, I know how absurd this all sounds. Where the heck was it supposed to progress to with me being in the ninth grade?? When you are a teen in the feels, there's no real logic. At least there wasn't any for me. The entire scope of our relationship was talking on the phone and sending each other letters. Yes, letters by mail, not to be confused by email. We are talking pony express here. It was nice and all, but it never felt real. Or, at the very, least it wasn't enough.

At the same time, Guy #2 was very real. We shared the same space, I could talk to him, cut up and laugh with him, and I was starting to seriously entertain the idea that we might hookup. The idea of hooking up with Guy #2 should have set off alarms inside my head. He was five years older than me. By the time you're thirty or so a five year age gap isn't much to talk about, but when you're fourteen or fifteen, it's a different story.

My dating life was a circus. I was pretty busy trying to figure me out and what I really wanted. Mind you, all the while keeping my options open and exploring my possibilities. I was dating Chris via telephone, pursuing or exploring where my crush might go as far as Guy #2 was concerned, and when I got really bored, I would dust off the list and make a few calls.

On one of those days while making calls from the list, I called this guy named Mike. He was different from the other guys I called. All the phone numbers that I had ever called from the list were all random, out of the blue phone calls. None of the guys knew me or why I was calling. None of them had ever seemed bothered or concerned by that either. All of the other guys just went with the flow, and before you knew it, we'd be talking like we were long lost friends. Mike, however, was not interested in talking to me. He asked me how I got his number, and I told him it was from my friend Ericka. He said he didn't know her, didn't know how she got his number and he didn't want to talk to me.

I laugh every time I think about it. The entire thing was just crazy. In the past, if I called a guy and I didn't like his voice, I didn't like him. I simply crossed his name off the list. It wasn't a big deal, there were plenty of numbers on the list. A few weeks went by and I went back to the list. Somehow, his number hadn't been crossed off, and I didn't realize it until he picked up the phone. This time he had a little more time for me, maybe he was bored he didn't have anything to do, or maybe he was curious. He asked me again how I got his number, and when I told him Ericka, he maintained he didn't know her. It was a decent conversation and he had a great voice.

Now I've added someone new to the mix. Let's keep it straight. I was crushing on and hanging out with Guy #2, dating Chris and now "talking" to Mike.

Mike and I went from talking a couple times a week, to talking a few times every single day. The more I got to know him the more I really liked him. His telephone voice was so sexy. It didn't hurt that he is Puerto Rican, and when he spoke to me in Spanish, it made me feel some type of way. It didn't matter that I had no idea what he was saying, it was all in the delivery. I was hooked. I loved that he wasn't anything like the guys I'd talked to in the past; he wasn't like Chris either. The others were all so quick to say "Be my girlfriend", Mike was not. I didn't get it. He seemed to like me, he was flirty when we talked on the phone, but he just would not ask me to be his girlfriend.

One day we were talking, and we had been talking for maybe two months or so (which is a lifetime in teenage dating years), and I asked him why he hadn't asked me to be his girlfriend. He just kind of chuckled, and said he would have except he knew that I was talking to his homeboy, Chris. Actually, he explained that Chris wasn't just his homeboy, but was his next door neighbor. That part… then he hung up.

I was shocked. Stunned. Shook.

Mind blown by this revelation. I didn't even know what to do or say. All that time that we had been talking, and I never once mentioned Chris; neither had he. How long had he known? Did Chris know, too? Were they talking about me? Why didn't he say something sooner? What was his end game?

I had all these questions, but Mike had hung up on me already.

Mike stopped taking my phone calls, so I started writing him letters. He eventually took one of my phone calls, and I poured out my teenage heart, explaining to him how everything is different with him, which was true because I really liked him, and that I was going to break up with Chris so that he could be my boyfriend.

Even before I had ever set eyes on Mike, there was just something about him that I couldn't shake. Keep in mind, I hadn't met him yet, but his voice was everything. His game was strong, he was confident and uncomplicated and he always said exactly what was on his mind. I knew I had to break things off with Chris so I could be with Mike.

Breaking up with Chris was harder than I thought. It turns out it wasn't easy for me to hurt someone's feelings who had done nothing wrong. I just wanted to end the relationship so I could be Mike's girlfriend. When I talked to Chris, he was nice and kind, I just couldn't break up with him, so I didn't. I called Mike and I just didn't bring it up. No problem right? Wrong, because he did.

> **Mike:** Did you break up with Chris?
>
> **Me:** Not yet, I just don't know how to…
>
> **Mike:** Oh you don't?, Let me show you
>
> -----"click"----

He hung up on me. This was classic Mike. Anytime he wanted to make a point with me he would just hang up. So rude!

I refused to lose Mike simply because I couldn't manage to break up with Chris. I knew it would be uncomfortable to be honest with Chris, but it's what I had to do to move forward with Mike. I paced the floor. I rehearsed what I would say to him with the most appropriate tone of voice. Finally I got up the nerve to call Chris and ended it. He didn't let go easy, but he wasn't shocked to find out I was ending it with him, because I wanted to be with Mike. I guess they had discussed me. If that wasn't enough, I was still fooling around with Guy #2 from my neighborhood.

At the time I didn't think it was a big deal. It was normal to have sex with somebody you weren't dating. In my mind you weren't a "hoe" unless you were sleeping with multiple people and I wasn't so, I thought I was doing pretty good. Mike and I did make it official that we were boyfriend and girlfriend, but we still hadn't met in person. It was emotionally real for me, but I was still looking to occupy my time when we weren't on the phone.

I know this seems messed up, but what type of decisions do you expect me to make? I was still in the ninth grade for crying out loud! It's clear I had no idea what it meant to be in a serious committed relationship.

I turned 15 years old over Christmas break of my freshman year in high school. During the break my mother finally gave me permission to wear make-up and I could officially "date". There were a pile of stipulations, addenda and "you better not....", but the fact remained I could date out in the open. The moment I was able to have an official boyfriend I told her all about Mike. Well, not ALL about him, I didn't tell her his age or that we had already started "dating" over the phone, but I gave her a few details. She was probably relieved at the fact Mike lived thirty minutes away. She didn't expect we would get too serious or get into much trouble considering the distance.

Once Mike and I could "date" out in the open we talked on the phone even more, I wrote him letters and sent him pictures. I wanted him to know how I looked, but I never got any pictures from him. I didn't care one bit. His voice and his talk game was the truth. The way he always knew exactly what to say and how to say it was more than enough for me.

After about four or five months of talking and writing letters, we finally got a chance to meet face-to-face. My mom had to go to Daytona to run a few errands and agreed to take me by Mike's house to pick up a gift he had for me. Mind you, it was a Christmas gift from a few months prior that he never had the opportunity to deliver.

I was scared, nervous and excited all at the same time. While I would only be allowed to stay long enough to say "hi" and pick up my gift, we were both so excited to see each other, we would gladly take whatever we could get.

The moment of truth had arrived! Pulling up to Mike's house we moved in slow motion. My throat went dry, my palms got all sweaty, apparently my entire body switched to auto-pilot, and decided it was going to do whatever it wanted to do, and all I could think was "I hope he thinks I'm cute."

Before I could knock on the door it opened and there he was. The first thing I noticed was his hair, there was just so much of it. A mountain of enormous brown curls stacked atop his head and he had so much hair on his face he could be confused with a grizzly bear. He was big and tall with a face covered in freckles. So many freckles! He had the most gorgeous brown eyes shaded by the longest eyelashes I'd ever seen on a man. Mmm.

Apparently, I had freckle fever that lay dormant until I met Mike. I was totally enamored with his freckles and eyes. When he described himself to me over the phone months ago he said he was Puerto Rican, but I didn't remember him mentioning the freckles. I never imagined a Puerto Rican guy with freckles either. He also understated how big and tall he was. Or maybe my imagination had failed me. Compared to me and the other guys I knew, he was a giant. He was approximately 6'1 and maybe 275-300 lbs. At the time, I was about 5'3" weighing in at about 125 lbs. He was so good looking and his size made him seem very manly. I loved the way he towered over me. He did not disappoint. Our visit only lasted 10 minutes, but that was all I needed. I was sure. It was Mike, and it would always be Mike.

I am not sure how he felt in that moment. He held my hands, looked down at me and smiled. He told me I looked nice, then he brought out the gifts. He handed me this small, white teddy bear in a red sweater with a white heart stitched to the center. He motioned for me to examine the bear closer and I noticed the gold hoop earrings in its ears. They were for me. I was smiling from ear to ear. I thanked him and told him I wouldn't be able to wear the earrings because I was allergic to the nickel in costume jewelry.

This made him laugh. He told me he knew that because I told him about it when we first starting talking so he made sure the earrings were 14k gold. I was impressed. Not just with the earrings, but the fact that he was actually paying attention to and remembering the details of our phone conversations from months prior. He then handed me another gift. This gift was for me to give to my mother. I gave him a puzzled look as I opened the bag. I pulled out a Simon. You know, the game with the lights and the sounds you have to mimic? My momma loved that game and I had wanted to get her one for Christmas a few months ago, but didn't have the money. Apparently, he remembered that too and bought it for me to give to her.

This dude right here had ALL the game! After the first successful meeting we were granted permission to see each other in public places with a chaperone over the next few months. We went on our first date to the Volusia Mall. We walked around the mall going from store to store holding hands or with his hand on the small of my back. He sat with me while I got my nails done he bought me a few pairs of shoes. I went into Rave, a clothing store, and he followed. I was standing in an aisle looking through a rack and I turned to look at him. He pulled me close and slowly lowered his face, pressing his lips to mine. I had never been kissed like that before. It was slow, his lips were hot and his tongue felt amazing. How did he do that? I played it cool, but my heart was pounding, I was smiling like an idiot and I felt the blood rushing to a southern region in my body if you get my drift. Our date ended with a quick bite to eat from Burger King.

We continued to talk two and three times a day. I always wanted to talk to him and wished he lived closer. I would have cut things off with Guy #2 if he did. We just didn't get to see each other often at all.

He was everything a girl could want in a guy. He showered me with compliments, encouraging words and a listening ear. He listened to me ramble on about whatever problem I was having with family or drama with my friends. He was also an amazing kisser, which didn't hurt at all. He was definitely a keeper.

CHAPTER THREE

Pregnant at 15, Yep.

I had sex with Guy #1 in the seventh grade, and now in ninth grade I was having sex with Guy #2. I never held any delusions that either of them were my "boyfriend". Guy #2 was just a guy I talked to and had sex with; I wasn't his girlfriend, and truth be told I wasn't bothered by that. As I look back from this stage of my life, it is a big deal and I wonder what I was thinking. Why didn't I have a better view on what sex was all about? Why was I not emotionally invested with the people I chose to share myself with?

Where had this line of thinking or detachment come from? I'm not sure.

My momma didn't talk to me about sex. Not really. I don't remember talks about the importance of waiting until I was married, or that sex was something special and I should treat it that way. It was something that was accepted, expected, it was a given. It was a given that I would have sex before I was married. The only request she made was that I talk to her about it BEFORE it happened, so she could put me on birth control. I didn't think it would be that easy. I thought if I told her what I planned to do, and with who, I would never see the light of day again. I would not fall for that trap, so instead, I hid it from her. She didn't tell me it was okay to have sex, or at what age it was acceptable, but it was like she didn't imagine it was likely that I would wait until marriage. As a parent, I get it. The odds seem to be stacked against us. We live in a sex charged society, and the idea that adults, let alone teens, will wait seems to be an antiquated notion.

This is a cautionary tale for young people; this and a laundry list of other perfectly good reasons why you shouldn't be having sex so young. I had an emotional attachment to Mike, but was involved sexually with Guy #2. I didn't even enjoy it. And I can honestly say I had no idea why I kept doing it. I thought this must just be how sex is. It wasn't horrible, but it wasn't enjoyable, either. It was like walking on a treadmill, or doing laundry; just very mundane. I just didn't see what all the fuss was about.

Reflecting as I write this book, I wonder why I didn't stop to question that. I never stopped to ask myself why I was giving myself to someone who never claimed me as his girlfriend, someone that I didn't want to be claimed by, when I had someone I actually liked. I didn't even understand my own feelings, and I was too young and stupid to realize it then. I didn't know what it meant to be in a relationship. I wasn't prepared for the consequences of having sex.

I wasn't prepared for an STD or getting pregnant. I wasn't prepared to handle what it might do to my reputation, my self-image or how it might impact how I valued myself, if I continued like this. I didn't think about those things at the time.

I had sex with Guy #2 a handful of times, maybe more, but each time I couldn't wait for it to be over. I didn't understand how the feelings I had leading up to having sex were so, intense, but the act itself was always a let down. It was living out the definition of insanity, doing the same thing over and over expecting for it to be different from the time before. I think I might have been in disbelief. I mean, people were fighting over it, fought for it, waged wars, and some men spent their hard earned money all in the name of sex. It HAD to be better than this. Boy was I wrong.

My mess of boy confusion and teenage shenanigans came crashing to a stop when I got caught skipping school. My friends and I would sometimes skip school, and we would hang out with Guy #2 and his friends. My education was still important to me, but I realized I didn't need to be in class EVERY day to be educated. I could just get the notes and assignments from a classmate and I would be fine. The school had an automated message that would call the house to let my momma know I had missed a class. I would simply intercept the call and pretend like it was a friend on the other end, and then delete the call from the caller ID. Easy. With such a great system, how could I get caught? Well, a friend's mom found the book bags we stashed near her house, and drove them down to the high school. Yet another downside of growing up in a small town.

Caught red-handed, I had two decisions to make. I could tell my mother the truth, confess to hanging out and having sex with an older guy, and maybe have "the talk" that was very long overdue. Or, I could keep the details of my day to myself and deal only with my inevitable punishment for skipping school. I chose the lesser of the two evils, skipping school because I couldn't even imagine the aftermath of confessing the full truth.

After getting busted for skipping school, I didn't talk to Guy #2 as much. He was still around, I saw him and we shared a few words, but it was definitely not like it was before, which was fine with me. Something had shifted in my head; the allure was gone. I'm not sure how he felt, and didn't care enough to ask. I was wise enough to know we were never a couple, so a breakup conversation wasn't necessary.

Once the dust settled and I was back to normal, no more skipping school or having sex with Guy #2, I felt free, unburdened and lighter somehow. I didn't have all the emotional conflicts waging war in my head like before; I was finally able to focus on school and Mike. Even with everything that went on between me and Guy #2, Mike and I never stopped talking. I never told him what I was up to, but I assumed he had a few things he was keeping from me too. Nevertheless, Mike and I were getting closer; my feelings for him were getting stronger everyday.

One afternoon, I was laying across my bed, staring up at popcorn ceiling as I sang along to the song blaring from my stereo...

> *"It's like raiiiian on your weddiiiiing day, issa free riiiiiiiide when you've already paid, it's the good adviiiiiiiiiice....."*

I just allowed my thoughts to go wherever they wanted as I sang along mindlessly. As I lay there singing and thinking about nothing in particular, I realized I couldn't remember the last time I had my period. I didn't freak out. It wasn't that I didn't have one, I just couldn't remember it. I sat up slowly and stopped singing. I reached over to the nightstand and turned the knob on the stereo to lower the volume of the music. I couldn't think and sing at the same time, and I couldn't stop singing as long as the music was playing. I sat silently, now with my legs dangling over the side of the my twin bed.

I closed my eyes and tried to see the events of the previous month with my minds eye. I searched my mind to find an event, or a day, that was ruined by the pain and agony that was my cycle. It was not something that was easily forgotten, but it seemed like somehow I had forgotten it. I sat for what seemed like forever trying to remember. From the first time my cycle reared its ugly head in the sixth grade, it made a faithful, 7-day long appearance each and every solitary month, like clockwork. I thought long and hard. How long had it been? I was standing now, pacing the small room. My hands were starting to sweat and my heart was pounding.

How long had it been? Think girl, think! One, two...oh dear LORD! It had been three months, THREE months since my last period. THREE MONTHS! You have got to be freaking kidding me right now! How did this happen??? I stopped pacing and just stood in the middle of the room trying to breath. What happened to all the oxygen? I was having difficulty breathing. My heart was pounding in my ears now, which made it difficult to hear my own thoughts. Had I really gone three months without a period?

I walked to my nightstand, opened the small drawer and pulled out my calendar. Why hadn't I thought to just pull it out in the first place? I held the small calendar in my hand, knowing it was not going to set me free. I turned the pages slowly, looking for the little red checks. January....yes, February.....yes, March.....nope, April.....uh, May.... "oh my goodness". It was May, May 19th to be exact, and still no period. Panic was beginning to set in. Could I be pregnant? I mean, it was possible. Guy #2 and I never used protection. How stupid was that? So stupid! Wait, there could be another explanation. Stress?, I thought to myself. Yes, that's it. Stress. I read somewhere once that stress could cause you to miss your period. I didn't know if it would last for three months, but it was a viable and logical explanation to the missing of my period. I didn't feel pregnant. Yeah.. "I'll take stress for $500, Alex."

Things had been kinda stressful for the past few months, and stress can cause you to miss your period, so that must have been it. I pushed the possibility of pregnancy right out of my head. The crisis was over. I wasn't pregnant, and that was the end of that. With that problem solved, I turned the music back up and took my place on the bed singing to the ceiling. I felt this wave of relief. I could breathe again, and my heart was now beating at a normal volume. I wasn't as stressed as I had been, so I would see my cycle return the next month, or so I thought.

A few weeks passed, school was out and life was good. One evening, as I was getting ready to take a shower, I felt water drop on my leg. I looked up to see if the ceiling was leaking, but I didn't see anything. I turned the shower on, and stood outside of the tub as I waited for the water to warm. Then, I felt a second drop. It didn't look like water. With my index finger, I wiped it from my leg and raised it eye-level to better examine it. It wasn't water, but I wasn't sure what it was. I turned my head again to the ceiling to investigate. Still nothing. As I turned my attention back to my leg, I realized where the liquid was coming from. It was coming from me. My body. My breasts were leaking.

Everything stopped. Sound. My heart. My breathing. Everything. I was brought back to reality by another drop from my breast onto my leg. The sound of the shower and everything else around me came rushing back. I gasped for air, as my lungs were in desperate need of it.

As I blinked back tears, my knees just gave out. I looked down at my stomach. It was a little plumper than it had been, and when I touched it, it wasn't soft like I'd enjoyed too much Gary's Chicken, it was firm. I stood up and turned the shower off. Wrapping my body in a towel I headed back to my room, closing the door behind me. I stood in front of the mirror and slowly removed the towel. I wanted to look at myself in the mirror, but the tears blurred my vision. I blinked them away and felt them roll slowly down my face. I looked again to the mirror. I stood there staring at my naked body, a body that had betrayed me, a body that seemed foreign to me now. My eyes went straight to my belly. I slowly turned to the side.

Now, as I stood there taking in my profile, I began to question myself. How had I denied this for so long? How had I not noticed? My breasts were swollen. Not that they were ever small, but they were heavier than they had been. They, like my belly, were firmer too...unusually so. I looked down at my stomach and knew that there was a baby in there, and no amount of denial could change that. I couldn't hold back the tears any longer. Through tears, I reached for my night clothes, slowly put them on, then carefully lowered my body to the floor. I grabbed my pillow from the bed, and pushing my face into it, I began sobbing. I couldn't cry out because my momma would hear it and come running. What would I say to her? The thought of having to tell my mother brought on another wave of tears, and more sobbing. I lay on the carpet in the fetal position, clutching the pillow to my face, sobbing uncontrollably until there were no tears left. I climbed into bed, turned the pillow dry side up, and went to sleep. I was exhausted.

Why did I get pregnant by Guy #2? How did I let this happen? I don't know. I was just so blind and impulsive. I didn't feel the same way about him as I felt about Mike; sex was just sex. It wasn't all the time, maybe a handful of times..maybe. I needed to tell Mike. I knew that would be the end of us. I couldn't blame him, but I didn't want it to be over. It had been a couple of months since I had sex with Guy #2 and the last few months with Mike were amazing. We weren't having sex and still had only seen each other twice, but I was dedicated to him. I wanted to be all his, no longer sharing my body with anyone else. It didn't matter that my past actions had caught up with me and I was pregnant. I called him the next morning and just said what I needed to say.

> **Mike:** Hello
>
> **Me:** Hey
>
> **Mike:** Wassup
>
> **Me:** Well.... When I started talking to you I was having sex with this dude, we haven't done anything in a few months, but I just found out I'm pregnant.
>
> **Mike:** You pregnant?
>
> **Me:** Yeah..
>
> -----"click"----------

I wasn't surprised he hung up and I didn't think he would forgive me, but I had hoped for an opportunity to tell him how sorry I was, how it didn't mean anything and that I wanted to be with him. I tried calling him back, but he didn't answer.

I needed to figure out what I was going to do. I closed my eyes and grabbed my belly. It knew it wasn't a dream, but I needed a reminder and a reality check. I had no intentions of ever telling my momma, which left me with only one choice, abortion. I waited for my momma to leave for work, then I went straight to the 90's version of Google, the phone book. I sat on the couch with the massive book in my lap, and went straight to the yellow pages. A....for abortion. There were many to choose from, but I didn't have a preference, I just needed to find one and make an appointment.

I called the first one on the list. I explained my situation, I was 15 and pregnant, I didn't want my momma to know and I couldn't stay overnight. The lady was very nice, encouraged me to tell my mother (NOT gonna happen lady), and set the appointment for me. It wasn't going to be free, but that was okay because I had already started working that summer and had a few hundred dollars saved up. Next step was to get a ride.

I called Guy #2, told him I was pregnant, it was his and I wasn't keeping it. He didn't question whether or not he was the father, and didn't give his opinion on my decision to end the pregnancy, either. I told him I needed a ride to the clinic, my friend would go with me and no one would ever find out. We could both go about the business of living our lives. He agreed to give me a ride. He didn't have a car of his own, but would borrow one.

Just imagine, I had a human life growing inside of me, yet I didn't have the simplest things, like a car or a license. Actually, I didn't even know how to drive! I hadn't taken drivers education yet. I didn't even have a driver's permit. I was just finishing up ninth grade, going into tenth. Instead of checking off books from the summer reading list, I was sneaking behind my mothers back, planning to terminate a pregnancy because I was too afraid to admit what I had done.

I know that people have abortions for many different reasons, for me it was because I didn't want my mother to ever find out. I guess mother's intuition trumped my ability to cover up the biggest secret I had ever kept, because one morning, out of nowhere, my mother asked me point blank:

Momma: *Are you pregnant?*

Me: *No.*

Momma: *Well you sure are sleeping a lot, and your belly is looking a little pregnant.*

Me: *Maybe I need to lay off Gary's fried chicken, but I am not pregnant.*

Momma: *Okay, time will tell.*

Me: *Yep.*

Instead of coming clean, I held on to the lie. I knew I would be getting the abortion soon, so why mess everything up? If all went according to my plan, I would have the abortion and she would never know.

Although I didn't have any of the basic necessities of adult life, I had taken charge of the situation. This was my body, my pregnancy and my decision. I made the appointment with the clinic. I made sure that I had enough money to pay for the procedure. I had also made arrangements to spend the night at a friends house once everything was completed. I had a well thought-out plan, and all I needed from Guy #2 was for him to secure transportation and keep his mouth shut. Which seemed simple enough.

I was feeling overwhelmed by the situation and I wish I could talk to Mike. I had made several attempts to contact him after our last conversation, but he wouldn't take my calls. I decided to give it another try. I'm not sure what made him answer the phone this time, but I was so glad he did. I didn't know how much I missed him until I heard his voice on the other side. I just cried. To my surprise he didn't hang up. He just listened to me cry. As I finished I told him how I felt, how I missed him and wished we could start over. Turned out he missed me too. He asked me what I was going to do about the baby. I told him about my plan to have an abortion. If he had an opinion or any thoughts about my decision he kept them to himself. He only said to let him know if I needed anything and that he was there for me. I was so grateful to have him back in my life.

I had everything planned so precisely, because I knew I didn't have any time to waste. I was pretty far along, maybe 18-20 weeks. My window of opportunity was diminishing quickly. I could not afford for anything to go wrong. The only piece of the puzzle that I had no control over was transportation. Again, I left this up to Guy #2, who assured me that he would take care of it. He had one job. ONE.

On the day of my appointment, I was at my friends house as planned, waiting for Guy #2 to pick me up. On pins and needles, I waited in vain. The minutes ticked by like a death march, and there was still no car out front or phone call. I had a plan, I had a good plan, and as each minute passed by, I was watching this plan crumble down around me. It was obvious something had gone wrong.

He called to say he couldn't get the car. His cousin asked him what he needed the car for, and like an idiot, he told her. She and my older sister were really good friends when they were in high school, and she didn't feel right about helping him. More small town awesomeness. She told him he needed to tell his grandmother, whom he lived with, and that I needed to tell my momma too. Instead of calling me to tell me his new plan, he just went home and told his grandmother. Now they were both on their way to my friend's house, whose mother was home and completely in the dark about the entire situation.

When he finally showed up, head hung and defeated, grandmother in tow, I was so disgusted. I was 15, ready to do what needed to be done, and he was 20 and unable to do something as simple as getting me a freaking ride to the clinic. Like, really dude??

The secret I had hidden away, safe from prying eyes, the information I had shared with the only friend that needed to know and would never tell a soul, had been shared without my permission, with two people who were destined to expose me. If I wasn't so numb I would have been livid. Numb and detached, I listened to his grandmother demean me without reply. What was there to say? I listened as she said things like:

> *"My grandson is going to the military to make something of himself, and when he comes back to town you'll be walking down the street with ya lil' baby, pointing at him saying: "there's ya daddy."*
> *"Are you sure it's even his?? Daddy's maybe, momma's baby!"*
> *" You need to flush this one down the toilet."*

I didn't realize my friend's momma had been listening from her room, but at the last comment, she came storming out. She stood between me and his grandmother and told her she was dead wrong for speaking to me that way. I was only 15, and she should be having this conversation with my mother. She told her they needed to leave, and as she closed the door behind them, she turned and looked at me and told me to call my momma, or she would.

The cat was out of the bag, and I had to call my mom to tell her. Dialing the phone, I noticed the time and made a mental note that I had missed my appointment, and my plan, the well thought-out, perfectly coordinated and fool proof plan, had failed miserably.

I called my momma and told her I needed to tell her something. I faced my biggest fear, out of necessity, not desire, but either way, I did tell my mother. I told her I was pregnant and that I was having an abortion. She was shocked, stunned and probably a little confused too. She had suspected the pregnancy, but she didn't expect for it to be Guy #2's. The only guy I talked about was Mike, so she just assumed we had figured out a way to sneak and hookup, and that the baby was his. The truth was, Mike and I had never been together like that. I liked him a lot, even felt like I might love him, but we just hadn't gotten to that place yet. Anyway......

That weekend my entire family came over. All the women came by to talk to me about not having an abortion. With patience and love for me and my unborn baby, they told me: "That's not what we do. You know we will help." The truth was, even though I never wanted my momma to find out, once she did know, I still didn't want to have the baby. I had already gone school shopping; this was the first year I could wear a halter top. I didn't want to get fat, I didn't want to have stretch marks, nothing about being pregnant or having a baby was appealing to me.

Despite everyone's best efforts, well wishes and stories about the joys of motherhood, nothing helped. I had earnestly listened to my aunts, my grandmother, cousins, and even my mother. I just did not want to keep this baby. My mind was made up. I would follow through with the abortion.

I called the clinic back myself, and rescheduled the appointment. This time, instead of waiting on Guy #2 to get a car, Motherdear, my grandmother, was going to go with me. My momma had to work and while Motherdear didn't agree with it, she wouldn't have me go alone, either.

The morning of the appointment, I was dressed and waiting to leave. I needed to put a letter in the mail before we left. When I crossed over from the living room to the porch, it was like an invisible veil have been lifted from my eyes. It felt like a dam break had given way in my chest, and emotions flooded my heart and mind. l fall short at describing it now. In that moment, I realized what was closed off from me before. This precious life inside of me was not a "problem" I needed to fix. It wasn't something I needed to get rid of. The minute I crossed over that threshold, the "thing" inside of me became a baby, and not just any baby, it was MY baby. I was breathless, overcome with emotions and tears, gasping for air and I grabbed my belly at the realization of what I was planning to do. I was about to get rid of my baby, and everything inside of me was opposed to that idea, the moment the "veil" was lifted.

I walked back into the house a totally different person. Hand on my belly, tears all over my face and my mind made up. All eyes were on me as I said loud and clear "I changed mind, I am keeping my baby." All the women in the room exclaimed with praises of joy and excitement. My mother looked relieved and happy. Surrounded by these beautiful strong women, I felt safe and sure in my decision. What touches my heart as I sit here and type, is that the "crisis" that we had averted was never the pregnancy, but rather, the abortion. I know there are many teenage girls who faced the exact opposite reality, and who are presented with a completely different set of options. It is for this, and perhaps a million other reasons, that I am eternally grateful for my mother, Motherdear, and the women who came to encourage and support me. I still went to a clinic with Motherdear later that same day, but this trip was to get me and the baby checked out, and to make sure everything was ok.

I felt good about the decision to keep the baby, but I had to tell Mike and I wasn't sure how he would take it. We were finally back together and I didn't want to mess that up.

Mike: Hello

Me: I decided to keep my baby. I just couldn't go through with it.

Mike: Really?

Me: I know you didn't sign up for this so I just wanted to call you and let you know. I wish things had turned out differently. I love you.

Mike: Yeah, me too. I'll try to stick it out with you and the baby see how it works out.

Me: I appreciate that, but I'm about to be a mother. I can't do the "try" thing, real daddy's don't stick around and I can't have my kid coming up calling a new dude "daddy" everytime I decide to date. I get it though.

Mike: I can't make you promises like that.

Me: I know.

Mike: Alright, I guess that's that then.

Me: bye

As I hung up the phone, I felt deep sadness. I was in this by myself. I wasn't a stranger to single parents or teen parents. I was raised by them... momma, Motherdear, Grandma, Aunties...yep. I just never thought I would be one.

As expected in a small town, the news traveled fast. Everyone and their cousin knew I was pregnant, and the rumor mill ramped up to full speed with questions and speculation about who the baby's father was. Guy #2 and I were never actually an item, so we were never seen alone together, always in a group. Mike had come to visit once, and that was all it took. His size and ethnicity wasn't easily forgotten. We walked around town, so quite naturally, everyone swore it had to be Mike's baby.

Summer came to a fast end, and it was almost time to return to school. One night while sitting in my room, on my bed..singing no less, the phone rang. I answered.....

Me: Hello

Mike: I'm in

Me: What are you talking about?

Mike: You, me, the baby...I'm in, I'm all in

Me: you sure?

Mike: yeah

Me: (crying) I love you.
Mike: I love you too.

Words can't really describe the happiness I felt as Mike and I were back together again. Once he said he was in, he meant it. He started going to doctors appointments with me when he could. Whenever we talked he always asked about the pregnancy. We were seeing each other more often now.

I loved him with everything I had in me. We kissed a lot, but it never went any further than that. One evening I was hanging out with him, at his house...in his bedroom and we were kissing like we had done a million times before. I wanted to have sex with him. He had made it clear he wanted it also, but I just wasn't ready. It's like I knew it would be different with him, not knowing it could be different. The moments leading up to that first time were hot and heavy, but I had no expectations for the act itself. I would just do this with him because I loved him and I felt like he deserved it. I will spare you the details, but let me say this. I no longer wondered why people were obsessed with it. I was wondering how it was they managed to do anything else if sex was this good. Like who has time for work, school, eating, hanging out when you could be doing this???

After the first time, it became a regular occurrence. Anytime we saw each other we made sure to participate in my new favorite activity. There was no more holding back. At the age of fifteen I had found the love of my life. I wanted to spend all my time with him, thought about him when we were apart and wanted to be touched by him so much so it still makes my heart race just thinking about it.

Going back to school with a baby bump was interesting, but uneventful. I returned all my super-cute clothes for oversized t-shirts and baggy jeans. I refused to wear maternity clothes; they were not as stylish as they are these days. I wasn't concerned at all about what the other kids would say about me being pregnant. You could be sure that my reputation preceded me. I was prepared to knock out the teeth of anyone who wanted to say anything to me about being pregnant. It wasn't necessary though. All my friends were still my friends, and everyone else I was cool with was still cool with me. It was good getting back into the routine of school, and I never let my pregnancy slow me down.

I continued to take honors classes, and found it easy to keep my grades up as long as I paid attention and did the required work. I was smart, so I didn't need a ton of study time. I was able to get the extra rest I needed now that I was carrying a baby. My teachers were shocked by the little bun in my underage oven. I think it came as a shock not only because I was so young, but partly because I wasn't "that type" of girl. I wasn't a wild child, dressing provocatively, getting into trouble with boys on campus. I wasn't an over-sexed teenage vixen. I wasn't even a "party" girl. By all accounts, I didn't fit the profile of a girl who would end up pregnant in high school. I wanted to say something, but every time it came up or when they would get that look on their face, I wanted to remind them: "You don't have to be wild or a party girl to end up like me, you don't have to be a problem child or promiscuous, you only need to have sex." All of the other qualifiers, stereotypes and labels were useless. It was sex, plain and simple.

There were several other girls in my school who were pregnant the same year. Our school administration, noting this spike in pregnancies, initiated a special program for teen parents. This program was put into place to accommodate us, and to offer additional support to help us maintain and achieve academic success while we were coping with the changes we would face as teen parents.

On January 4th I started having contractions. They started early that morning, but I wasn't sure it was time just yet. By the afternoon it seemed certain I would have the baby. I tried to reach Mike, but he was unavailable. He worked for a roofing company at the time and so I knew it would be difficult to locate him. This predates cellphones being as common as lollipops. I gave birth to my baby girl in a room filled with love and family. My momma, Grandma Caroline and Anterrius were all in the room when she came into the world. Mike arrived shortly after she was born, but before I could be cleaned up and transferred to my new room. He helped the nurse transfer me to a wheelchair and waited while she helped me get cleaned up.

That night he stayed in the hospital and slept on a little cot in the room with us. He had promised to be there for me and the baby a few short months ago and he had been. He chose to be a teen parent. Who does that? I mean, I was a teen parent, but I didn't choose it. He could have walked away, we weren't his responsibility, but he stepped up, he stayed. I hoped I would spend the rest of my life with him. Someone from the hospital came to the room to get my baby's name and to have me sign the birth certificate. I named her Micah after the love of my life. Even though we were young I knew he would always be there for Micah even if it didn't work out with us. He wasn't alone in accepting Micah as his daughter, he had his entire family behind him. His parents and his siblings welcomed me and Micah into their homes and their hearts without question.

CHAPTER FOUR

Love of My Life, Bae, My Boo.

Mike.

He was an amazing father! I didn't have much experience with great dads, but Mike was definitely showing me what it was all about. He wasn't just around he was involved and there is a huge difference. The first year of her life he made her an Easter basket full of candy she couldn't eat and a very loud toy bunny of some sort. It laughed loudly, lit up and flapped its long ears. Micah loved that thing. If I needed anything, clothes, money, diapers I could count on him. We were the family we decided we would be even though we didn't live under the same roof.

He was my go-to person for emotional support, for understanding, for love and affection. All of it. Now, we broke-up and got back together probably a thousand times because again, we were teenagers who had no real handle on our emotions or what it meant to be committed. He was still going out with his friends, getting into fights, getting arrested and I didn't want that for Micah. No matter what I said, I still couldn't let him go though. He was such a huge part of me and Micah's life. WE loved him. Despite his reckless behavior he was ALWAYS there for us.

I remember this time we were on a break. Micah was a little over a year old. I had this old car I was driving and there were these ants in it only I didn't know it at the time. I was driving down the street and Micah starts crying her head off. I turn around to see what the problem was and she was being attacked by ants. They were all over her legs. I pulled over and hopped out the car, barely putting it in park. I snatched her out of her car seat, also crawling with ants and brushed them away. When I told Mike about it he yelled at me and said that I needed to stop driving that car because it wasn't safe. I didn't really have much of a choice though. I bombed it instead. You know, the kind of bug bombs used in houses. Well, I used one in the car. I needed that car, I was still in school and I had a job so, just trashing it wasn't an option.

Mike calls me one day after the ant incident and asks me to come see him. We were still on a break so I wasn't trying to fall into his trap. I had almost no resolve when in his presence. A break would not last if I went to see him and he looked at me like I was a snack. Nope. I was serious about this break and no matter how sexy his voice was I was not going to see him.

> **Mike:** I got something for you and Micah, just come and get it, and ain't nobody trying to get back with you.
>
> **Me:** I'll come, but we are NOT getting back together you just won't do right.
>
> **Mike:** That's fine Taquesha just come and bring Micah with you.
>
> **Me:** Aight.

So I drive the thirty minutes to his house, butterflies in my stomach trying to pull it together. I loved him and not seeing him made it easier to tell myself he was not the right guy for me. Once I pulled up to that house and saw his face, whatever resolve I had was nowhere to be found. I was immediately overwhelmed by the need to reach out and touch him, by the need to be touched by him......I still had my lil' attitude though. I got Micah out of the car and she ran to be picked up by him. He smiled and held her in his arms, watching me as I approached slowly determined not to follow behind Micah although I desperately wanted to hop in his arms too. Little traitor, no solidarity.

> **Me:** (arms crossed) So what's up Mike?
>
> **Mike:** (unmoved by my attitude) let me show you what I got you.

> I followed him to the side of the house. He points to this white car in the driveway.

Me: (glaring at him) What's the gift Mike?

Mike: The car! I got this car for you and Micah come look! It's clean, A/C runs well, nice tinted windows, you like it?

Me: (holding on to that lil attitude) Where did you get this car? Did you steal it? Did you beat somebody up for it?

Mike: (laughing) no dumbass, I bought it....for you.

Me: (still with attitude for days) I can't afford no car payments so don't be giving me nothing I gotta pay for, that ain't no gift.

Mike: I bought this car for you and Micah, y'all don't need to be driving around in that raggedy car "The Prince" bought you.

"The Prince" is what he called my biological father, who outside of buying me the car in question hadn't done much of anything else for me. Prince Albert is his middle name and that really amused Mike, so much so that he still to this day refers to him as "The Prince". Now I am looking at this car, thinking about how even though we aren't in a relationship he cares so much about me and Micah he would get us a car...a nice car with no strings attached.

Me: I love you (I say this as I join Micah in his arms)

We obviously got back together at that point. Despite his shortcomings (the fighting, getting arrested) he was a guy that loved me and I loved him. I couldn't walk away from that. I was in twelfth grade and before I could graduate I decided to move out of my mother's house and in with Mike at his parents'.

Micah had been sick a lot and I missed several days of school a week as a result. I needed to take classes at the local community college if I was going to graduate on time. I didn't really have anyone to watch her while I went to school. My mother worked during the day. His mother didn't and she loved Micah too so she agreed to watch her while I was in class. It was easier if I moved in with them. It was Mike, Micah and I in a room together and before I could graduate from high school I was pregnant again. I'm sure that's not a big surprise, what else do young people do who live together? They have sex, and when it's good, they have lots of it.

Welp, now we needed to get our own place so we found this cute little two bedroom apartment we could afford, we moved in shortly after graduation. Things weren't perfect in our relationship remember, I was 18 years old with adult responsibilities. We argued, cursed each other out, and fought. Yes, I was still using my hands to express myself. He only got as physical as he deemed necessary in order to keep me off him. He held me down, pushed me away, but he didn't hit me. I know that's crazy, but we fought as hard as we loved, and no matter what, I knew I could count on him. He would always be there for us and he would protect us with his life. I knew he would never walk away from me and the kids.

After graduating from high school I didn't have any immediate plans to go to college. I had been accepted to a few, but for lack of knowledge I didn't go anywhere. I got a job and lived with Mike in our apartment. One evening we were hanging out in the living room with Micah, talking about nothing really. I lay on the floor, belly swollen with new life when he told me that he felt like he was holding me back from going to college. He understood I stayed to be with him, but he thought I should have gone because I was so smart.

I loved him for saying that. I HAD stayed in part because of him. Even though there were other factors. I didn't understand how financial aid work, so I didn't think I could afford to go to college. Even if the financing for college had been clearer I don't know if I would have packed up and walked away from him. I seriously doubted it. By the time I had graduated from high school, we had been together for about four years, had been parenting together for two and had lived together for almost 8 months and were expecting another baby. I just don't see me walking away or separating from that.

On February 15, 2000, He asked me to marry him. Of course I said yes and two months later I gave birth to our second child Michael, Jr. He didn't miss that one either. He had an office job so he was off the afternoon I went into labor. He picked me up from my nephew's birthday party and drove me to the hospital himself. He stayed by my side the entire time holding my hand or my leg, whatever the moment called for and encouraging me the entire time.

Even after lil Mike was born, he continued to encourage me to go to school. He was always encouraging me to dream big, telling me I could do anything. I wanted to be a lawyer and he thought I would make a great one because he said I loved to argue. I enrolled in the local community college and started taking classes.

Over the years we've had our ups and downs but my relationship with Mike is the strongest and deepest relationship I've experienced with another person.

I was going to school and planning a wedding. Our wedding date was set for March 17, 2001. On Friday, March 2nd 2001, we woke next to each other, in our second apartment together. It was much nicer and bigger than the first. Now that we had two kids we needed more space. He looked at me and said "Marry me today"!

> **Me:** Boy, stop playing we both have to go to work today and we get married in a couple of weeks.
>
> **Mike:** I'm serious.
>
> **Me:** (grinning like a fool) Okay!!

We called in to work, asked his mother to watch the kids, went to the courthouse and got married. I had this nervous but excited energy coursing through my body. I couldn't wait to be his wife. Mrs. Molina. I'd wanted this for what seemed like an eternity. After it was official, we called everyone and told them the wedding was off because we had just eloped.

Not everyone was as excited as we were. My mother was very upset and said that I would have to repay her for the wedding dress. She was also upset she wasn't there when we got married even though it was at the courthouse. I understood why she was upset, but it wasn't about anyone else. It was just about the two of us.

CHAPTER FIVE

Our Marriage Takes a Hit!

We didn't have a perfect relationship, but who does? Ours was full of highs and lows, peaks and valleys, smiles and tears. Our fights were terrible, but we always made up. We loved each other and were committed to our steady growing family. He was still going out with his friends at night while I spent my nights at home with the kids. This caused more fights, but Mike wasn't going to be staying home just because I wanted him to. He was grown and could do whatever he wanted, which he reminded me of often.

One night he stayed in and I fell asleep with him in the bed next to me. I woke up the next morning alone. Somehow, I knew immediately he had gone out after I was asleep. He had never done that before, and there was a feeling in my gut that something was wrong. I called his phone...no answer. I called everyone I could think of to see if he was with them. Nope. None of his friends had even heard from him. I was starting to panic. Here I was, a newlywed with two small children and a husband who was missing. I started calling local police departments to see if there was an accident or if something had happened to him. I finally called a police station that had some information.

He had been arrested for driving on a suspended license. I didn't understand.He was a good driver why did he even get pulled over? It didn't make sense to me. I asked for the details surrounding the arrest. I wanted to know what happened. The guy on the phone didn't answer my question though, instead he asked me one.

Operator: "Are you from Edgewater, FL?".

I wasn't from Edgewater, I was from the neighboring town, but I didn't see what that had to do with anything and I told him as much.

Me: What does the hell does that have to do with anything?

Operator: Your voice sounds so familiar, did you ever take a lamaze class at the clinic on Canal Street in New Smyrna Beach?

Me: uh...yeah...like 5 years ago.

Talk about "small world", turns out the officer had also been in that lamaze class and recognized my voice.

INSANE.

After we made that connection he encouraged me to come and get a police report. I got the police report and started reading it while in the police station. It stated that Michael was pulled over because he had dropped someone off and then drove through a parking lot and sat there. When they approached him he wasn't honest about who he was. The name he gave didn't match the DOB he gave with it. One officer went in the direction of the woman he had dropped off and the other stayed with him. He asked her to identify the guy who had just dropped her off and she said his name was Mike. They asked her how she knew, her response was, "that's what he told me."

I read that report a few times before tears made my vision blurry. Sitting alone, the buzz and chatter of the police department played in the background as my heart broke in ways I didn't know possible. Here in my hand, in black and white, no grey area, no possibility of uncertainty or ambiguity, my husbands transgressions were written in plain english, dates, names and locations. It was undeniable, irrefutable and completely conclusive.

I was devastated.

There were thousands of angry questions swirling through my mind. I needed answers, but it's not like I could ask Mike. He had been arrested and would remain in jail. Once I got my bearings and got myself together, I ran out of the police station like someone called in a bomb threat. I was furious and was ready to launch my own investigation. I left the police station and drove directly to the home of one of his closest friends. It was still early for them so no one came to the door. I didn't let that stop me. I went to the back door, which I knew was always open, and let myself right on in. I found the master bedroom and walked right in. His friend lay there with his girlfriend in bed while my yelling woke them both up. They thought something had happened to Mike, or to me. He began to get up and prepared to deal with it. When he realized Mike was the problem, he and his girlfriend denied any knowledge of Mike's infidelity. Not only did they deny knowledge of it they questioned the validity of my allegations.

Amy: "Quesha are you sure?",

Jake: "I think you might be wrong cause I never heard of her and Mike don't be f*&#ing with no hoes like that."

Me: Yeah right!!!! His a%^ is guilty it's right here on this police report so don't be lying for him now. Look just tell me where this hoe live so this b!#$ can come correct.

Jake: I already told you I don't know her and even if I did I sure as h#!# wouldn't tell you where she lives so you can get arrested. Nah...Mike ain't called you yet?

Me: No his a#$ ain't call yet

Jake: Just go back to the house and wait for him to call you.

Amy:. Quesha it'll all work out.

Me: F%$k y'all which ya lying a%$es!!

The investigation didn't end with "Jake" and his girlfriend. I am no quitter. I went on to interrogate two more of his closest friends and they all fed me the same line.

"It's not like Mike Quesha, ain't no way he cheated on you."

Obviously, they were doing what good friends do, covering for Mike's lying cheating behind. Why else was there some chick in his car? Why else did he leave our home, our bed and risk being arrested?

I started to realize the person I was most upset with was me. I didn't think I deserved it or any bullcrap like that, but I honestly never thought he would cheat on me. Never. Not because I was perfect or because I thought he was perfect, but because he had this habit of showing me the worst of him and then saying "deal with it". He didn't hide things from me.

I felt so stupid. This was the first time I felt like it was possible he had being playing me the entire time. I still believed he cared for me, but had he been faithful all these years? Probably not, that explained his willingness to take me back after I cheated on him with Guy#2. That was kid stuff though, I ended up pregnant as a result, but I was in the ninth grade this was different. We were married with children.

Just three months ago, we got married and now I was finding out he cheated or had been cheating on me for who knows how long. We had dated for almost five years before we got married. Why even bother marrying me if you didn't want to be with me??? Realizing he had cheated called into question the validity of the entire relationship. So many flashbacks of other incidents that made no sense popped into my head, I remembered times when I had called him in the past and his sister would lie and tell me that he wasn't there, when he was. So many little things now became bread crumbs all leading back to the scene of the crime. How hadn't I seen it before, was I that blind. Had I become one of those pitiful girls that was being played and was entirely too "in love" or too dense and pathetic to know?

I felt pathetic, I was embarrassed and ashamed.

Everyone knew how much Mike meant to me, now everyone would know how little I meant to him. It was humiliating. Society has a way of making you feel like you must have done something wrong if your spouse is unfaithful. That, of course, is a pile of dung. I drove to his mother's house. She was watching the kids for me. I sat in his old room sobbing, because I had so many questions, so much anger and so much shame.

Ring ring, ring ring....

It was the phone and I KNEW it was Mike. I picked it up "You have a call from Mike Molina from Volusia County Correctional Facility." I accepted the charges.

Me: Hey, what happened

Mike: I just went out driving around and then I got picked up on some bull$*#&

Me: Who were you with?

Mike: Nobody, I was by myself....

Well that was it. He told me that fast lie and I was on it like hot cakes. I started to ask him questions in rapid succession because I KNEW he was lying and he had no clue that I knew.

ME: WHY ARE YOU LYING TO ME? WHO IS MARTHA, BECAUSE THAT'S THE HOE YOU WAS WITH WHEN YOUR A$% GOT ARRESTED!!!

HOW DO YOU EVEN KNOW HER?

HAVE YOU BEEN FOOLING AROUND WITH HER THIS ENTIRE TIME?

WHY DID YOU EVEN BOTHER MARRYING ME IF YOU WAS GONNA JUST GO OUT AND HOOK UP WITH RANDOM HOES? YOU DIDN'T NEED ME FOR THAT!!!

He attempted to answer the questions, problem was there were no "right" answers to the questions. It didn't matter how he answered because nothing would change the betrayal.

Mike: I haven't been messing around on you it happened one time, it was just head.

ME: JUST HEAD? WHAT THE HE#@ IS THAT SUPPOSED TO MEAN? SO YOU JUST STUCK YOUR....

Mike: I don't know why I did it, I tried to wake you up before I went out, but you wouldn't get up.

ME: I KNOW YOU NOT TRYING TO BLAME ME FOR THIS!! SO SINCE I WAS SLEEP AT NIGHT LIKE YOUR A$$ SHOULD HAVE BEEN YOU DECIDED YOU WOULD LEAVE THE HOUSE WITHOUT YOUR RING AND GET HEAD IN A PARKING LOT?? YOU DESTROYED OUR FAMILY FOR SOMEONE YOU DIDN'T EVEN KNOW? YOU DIDN'T EVEN HAVE A RELATIONSHIP WITH HER?

Side note: It doesn't really matter if you had a relationship with the person or not at any rate you decided that what you were doing with that other person was more important than keeping your vows and commitments and that hurts. There is no way to minimize that hurt. I ended the call yelling and cursing at him.

I truly believe this situation tilled the ground in my mind and prepared it for depression to grow and take root. His cheating made me question my own worth. Part of me hated him and I hated myself because I still loved him and wanted to be loved by him. It felt like we weren't the couple I thought we were. I thought we were madly in love and just fought so much because we were both so strong willed. I never imagined he would cheat on me. Never.

I was mad, a soul stirring, hot headed, stark-raving-mad kind of mad. The upside to this horrible avalanche of devastation was that Mike was arrested and remained in the county jail. I am thankful for this now because only God knows what may have happened if I could have gotten my hands on him then.

Mike was not to be released for awhile, so me and the kids spent most of our time at his parent's house. It was so humiliating. I'm not sure why I felt humiliated...I hadn't done anything wrong, but I still felt this shame. I felt foolish for trusting him the way I did. I wondered if there were signs I missed, how did I miss them. I didn't know what I was going to do. He remained in jail for a few months which lead to him writing me letters. The sweetest, most heartfelt letters you can imagine.

I don't imagine any other types of letters are sent from jail though. Those months apart were hard on me and the kids. I missed him. I didn't deal with the feelings of betrayal, abandonment and the sadness I felt deep in my soul. I just moved on. By "moved on" I mean I stuffed those feelings down and tried to forget it. Not a great strategy, by the way, but it worked at the moment.

When he came home I was happy to see him and didn't want to talk about his cheating. It had been more than three months and I just wanted everything to go back to the way it was. We promised to be better to each other and shortly after he was released we became pregnant with our third child. Our new commitment to be kind to each other didn't last long. Sadly, things were worse than they had ever been before. At least they were for me. I had extreme self-doubt, feelings of worthlessness and I questioned my decision to stay, and what staying said about me. These were things I hadn't had to contend with before.

On July 4th, I gave birth to our baby girl Caira, the only child not named after him. I wanted to name her Michaela, but he said his name wasn't George Foreman and every kid didn't have to be named after him. Anterrius, actually gave us the name and we both liked it so we went with it. Her middle name came from Mike's favorite singer Sade, we both had a love for her music and she was probably conceived to the lyrics of Smooth Operator....lol. The birth of our third child did bring peace for a short time, but soon enough we were back at it.

We were on this cycle of arguing, fighting, me accusing him of cheating and him not caring enough to come home at a decent time. He would still hangout half the night sometimes letting the sun beat him home. I would cry during the night then greet him at the door with a swift attack.

He claimed he wasn't cheating, only hanging out getting drunk with his friends. He reminded me he was grown and didn't need me telling him what time to come home. I accepted this level of disrespect from him. He didn't take my feelings into consideration, he didn't care that his late nights always had me concerned about what he was doing and who he was doing it with. He did nothing to reassure me that he was faithful and committed to our marriage.

He actually turned it around on me. I needed to stop nagging him so much, I needed to trust him. If I didn't trust him I should leave him. This added a new layer of self-doubt and self-hate. I was always asking myself, why didn't I think I deserved better? Everyone around me, my friends, my family, his family all encouraged me to stand up for myself. If he couldn't treat me with respect I should leave him and they would all be there to support me.

Why did I stick around?

I didn't know. I loved him and I didn't want my marriage to be over. I wanted it to be better, but I didn't know if it ever would be. I wasn't ready to leave.

So I stayed…...

Fast forward about six or seven years, we relocated to North Carolina. Moving here changed the dynamics of our relationship. We didn't have any friends or family here so we had to rely on each other. It was great. We had a fresh start and it was us against the world for the first time in a long time. This was the man I had fallen in love with more than ten years ago. It was the happiest time of our lives together. We were even attending church regularly and he was leading the way in that too. It was like everything was finally coming together.

The sun was shining, birds chirping and flowers were blooming. Life was good. Then the clouds rolled in……..

CHAPTER SIX

It's Official, Marriage SUCKS!

I went to the doctor for a regular check up and while I was there she asked me if I wanted to be tested for STDs along with the pap smear. "Sure, why not?"

I knew the test would come back clean and it was included in the visit, which was covered by insurance. After a few days I received a call. The lady on the other end of the phone verified my identity and then begin to give me information.

Her: *Ma'am, you have tested positive for......*

I stopped listening after "tested positive," I had been having problems with my uterus, every year there were changes and so I had to get checked twice a year to make sure there was nothing cancerous.

I thought she was telling me I had cancer.

> **Me**: *I'm sorry, what did you say?*
> **Her:** *You tested positive for an STD….*
> **Me:** *(interrupting her) What's an STD?*
> *(thinking...never heard of that type of cancer before)*
> **Her:** *(voice FULL of annoyance with my question and my interruption) Ma'am a Sexually Transmitted Disease.*

I'd like to say for the record, I knew what an STD was, but at the time my life was going so well, we were living in lala land and I didn't think for a minute he was cheating on me (ironic, I know). Also, I really thought she was going to say I had cancer or something to that effect because my uterus had been quite troublesome.

I had stopped listening again.

Everything went quiet and seemed to move in slow motion. I could feel the tears making their way down my cheek. I was crumbling to the living room floor, my legs too weak to hold me. I could see Mike coming towards me, worry in his eyes. I held my hand up to keep him from getting too close.

> **Her:** *Ma'am are you married?*
> **Me:** *I am today.*
> **Her:** *Well, anyone you've been with will need to be tested.*
> **Me:** *not tested….treated.*

Her: *Ma'am we'll have to test him to see if he has contracted it...*

Me: Oh believe me he has it, where the hell do you think I got from??!

Her: We'll need to test everyone you've been with....

That brought me back.

Everyone I'D been with?!!!! No ma'am! My husband needed to be treated and NOT tested because he was the only one I'd been with. I ended the call and the Spanish Inquisition began.

Me: *How could you care so little about us that you would have unprotected sex with another woman?*

What if you had given me AIDS and would be taking me away from our small children?!!

I guess what they say is true, huh? Once a cheater ALWAYS a cheater?

You think I'm going to be dumb enough to stay with yo cheatin' a#$ again?

His response surprised me though.

Mike: *This wasn't me! I didn't cheat, it was you!*

IF you got something you didn't get that sh*\$t from me!

You the one out in the streets like a hoe!

Don't try to put this sh\$#t on me!

I knew it wasn't me. He was lying and I was going to leave him. I needed him to admit it though. I told him I could never forgive him for what he never admitted to, I would try to work things out if he confessed and stopped trying to blame me.

We sat in the living room crying as we watched our marriage and our new happy life disintegrate right before our eyes. He broke the silence.

Another confession.
He had cheated again, but it was during our separation when I was in college. This was more than two years ago and I called him on it. First of all, we weren't "separated" in the marital sense, he had moved during my last semester for work while I stayed in Tallahassee to complete my degree. We were still very much married. I won't lie, it was during a difficult and dark time in our marriage, but we were still married and this was NOT okay.

I was furious, not so much about the cheating, but the lying! It was impossible that it happened that long ago because I had no symptoms. I couldn't even remember what she said I had so I called the office back. They were closed for the day. I wanted to know if it was possible to contract whatever I had and not have any symptoms for two years.

I told him it was over. He apologized and begged me to stay. He professed his love for me and talked about how great things were with us now. I just couldn't. I felt like he never loved me. Never. Not sure how he got stuck with me, but he certainly wasn't happy. He always had a strong desire to be present in his kids life and so I felt like he was fighting for that and not actually fighting for me.

I was determined to leave. How could I stay? He had cheated on me twice and now I had an STD. How pathetic would I have to be to stay through that?

The next day I called the doctor's office, but she was unavailable. I was told she wanted to speak to me directly and would call in between patients. I spent the next few hours wondering what bad news she had for me. She finally called. She started with an apology. I could feel my stomach and heart begin to drop. She continued to explain to me there had been mixup and I didn't have an STD. My test came back normal and the lady who called me the day before had accidentally given me someone else results.

Me: *What the h#ll did you just say???*

You'd think I would have been relieved, but I wasn't. I was so pissed! What if I had killed him? What if he had killed me in a jealous rage? She had destroyed my happy home, not really, but I blamed her. Once I knew about the cheating I couldn't go back to not knowing...I wished I could though.

When I got home I told Mike about the results and the mixup. He was furious and relieved. Where did that leave us though? We didn't know. I shut him out emotionally and cried everyday. I hated him. I hated him for ruining our happy life. I was more hurt by his cheating this time than I was the first time. Who even knew that was possible?

I reached out to a woman I knew back home. We weren't close, but she had a very public case of infidelity with her husband that resulted in multiple children outside their marriage and she stayed. Need I remind you once again of the perks of a small town. Everybody knows your business or at least they think they know.

In my eyes, her ability to stay through that type of public betrayal (one she couldn't soon forget because there was an actual human being to stand as reminder), was a testament to her strength. All I wanted to do was run.

When I reached out to her I was surprised she was open to talking to me. We had never spoken on the phone before and nothing more than small talk in passing. We didn't have a relationship and all I knew of her struggle came from the ever talkin' streets of NSB. We didn't have a relationship which gave me no permission to question her about the intimate details of her marriage, but I was desperate and bold so I contacted her anyway.

She was so gracious. I cried on the phone with her, sobbed really and told her about my marriage and why I thought she would have some insight. She remained gracious. It was quite strange because before this conversation where we discussed the darkest parts of our private lives we had never entertained each other more than to speak casually and usually in passing. She had such a peace about her as she spoke to me. She never questioned why I called or asked me why I was prying into the intimate details of her marriage. Once I was all cried out she asked me two questions.

> **My Angel:** Do you love him?
>
> **My Angel:** Do you WANT to stay?
>
> **Me:** Yes, but the bible says I can leave him for this
>
> **My Angel:** it says you CAN it doesn't say you have to or that you should, you can choose to stay. It won't be easy and it's a long road back, but it's possible.

She prayed with me and told me to call her anytime. I decided to stay in my marriage because the truth was I knew things were different and they had been since we had moved to Charlotte. We were not the same we were before. I wanted to stay. I loved him then as much as I ever had if not more. Forgiveness, however, was not to be granted. I held on to the hurt and pain he caused me. The unforgiveness grew and blossomed into bitterness and depression. Such a beautiful disaster.

As I continued to cultivate a garden of mistrust and resentment in my heart we struggled to reconnect. We didn't split up, but there was no trust, no affection, it was a shell of a marriage. We didn't know how to rebuild, we didn't have the tools for healing. My wounds continued to fester while the sad darkness took root in my heart that would prove almost impossible to remove. We stopped going to church together and just went through the motions. We were distant and even the fire we once had when fighting had turned to ice.

About a year later, I reconnected with a guy from high school. We never had a relationship or anything, but we were friends (kinda) and I had a crush on him. Anyway...he sent me a friend request on facebook and when I realized it was him...I accepted. We did what people do on facebook which is nothing really.

I noticed he was atheist and at the time I was working on a magazine for teen girls. It wasn't going to be a Christian magazine, but it would have clear Christian values. I was doing research to see how different parent groups might respond. I reached out to him because he had a daughter in our target audience and I wanted to know what he might think about the magazine as an atheist parent.

He sent me his number and I called him. He was nice and respectful, just as I had remembered. We talked about the magazine and his thoughts, his concerns as a parent regarding a magazine with "Christian values" and that was pretty much the end of the shop talk. We then talked about high school and basically what we had been doing with our lives since we graduated. It was a pleasant conversation.

Somehow we ended up talking again, not really sure about what, but he was so easy to talk to it quickly turned into a daily occurrence. We talked everyday about any and everything or absolutely nothing at all. Mike would come home from work, but wouldn't come up to the apartment until well after dinner time. This made it easy to talk to him while I cooked dinner or while helping the kids with their homework. It still seemed innocent enough because we never talked about anything inappropriate.

One day, however, while helping the kids with their homework I realized I missed his call. Let me be clear...not that he had called and I didn't answer it, but I missed talking to him. I felt some type of way that we hadn't talked all day. I picked up my phone to call him and saw he had called me. He had called a couple times and sent me a text message. I felt butterflies in my stomach. It was at that moment I realized I had crossed a line. I was now the cheater. It may not have been a physical affair, but it was definitely an emotional one.

I wish I could say it ended there, but it didn't. I continued to talk to him because I liked how talking to him made me feel. My friends voiced their concerns, opinions and judgements. They all told me to stop talking to him. My response? I was tired of being cheated on maybe I would do the cheating this time. My closest friends Olivia and Shalander encouraged me to tell Mike how I was feeling and they were sure he would want to work on our marriage. They warned me not to do something I would regret..yada yada yada. I didn't want to hear that crap. I took their advice though and tried talking to Mike. I told him I missed him and needed more time and affection from him.

His response? "That's usually what hoes say before they cheat."

Is this dude for real??? It was clear to me he could see the signs, but he didn't care. He just wanted me to cheat so he could leave me and I would be the one responsible for destroying our family. Forget that fact that he had already cheated, twice!

His nonchalant-accustory response was all I needed to keep it moving. I continued to talk to my guy friend and initiated conversations that were team inappropriate. I liked it. I finally felt wanted. He lived in Florida so while I fantasized about cheating it was still safe...in my head anyway. Olivia was having a wedding in Florida, I was one of her matrons of honor (more irony..."honor"..I know) and would be only two hours away from the "faux boyfriend". I wanted him to be my date for the wedding. Mike didn't want to go and truth be told I didn't want him to go. I wanted to have a good time and we were still in a crappy place, all we did was argue and then freeze each other out.

I told Olivia my great plan and she shot it right down. I don't know what kinda friend she was not having my back. She laughed at my accusation and told me I had clearly lost my mind and would not be bringing another dude to her wedding besides my husband. My plus one was for Mike or I could come alone. She felt like I was crossing the line and had been for a while. She told me she and Shalander were worried about me because I was not acting like myself. I just rolled my eyes and mentioned how great it was that my two best friends were talking about me behind my back. She laughed again and said, "Well I'm telling you to your face now, so what?"

Well...he didn't accompany me to the wedding, but we did see each other. I was in Florida for a few days before the wedding and thought since I couldn't bring him as a date I could go see him. He might have been willing to come to me, but my friends would not have it. They were not going for that, no ma'am, no ham.

As God would have it something came up and we couldn't spend the day together even though that was the plan. I don't know what I would have done or how far I would have taken it. I will say this though. I realized I was capable of cheating on my husband. I blamed him for being flawed...and weak...unloving and selfish. That's why he cheated and that's why I NEVER would. Truth be told, if it were not for God keeping me I probably would have. I was overwhelmed with guilt and shame.

Mike and I talked when I returned home from the wedding. We needed to make a decision. Would we stay together or would we split up? I confessed to him all my transgressions. He said he figured as much. We sat and talked about how much we still loved each other and that we wanted to stay together and work on our marriage.

Forgiveness still would not come from either of us. We didn't heal, but we didn't walk away either. The worst part of all this is that our kids always had a front row seat to our dysfunction.

CHAPTER SEVEN

More Than I Could Bear

Toucan and I talked on a weekly basis. We talked about everything and everyone, including our own personal relationship problems. He liked Mike, they had formed somewhat of a relationship when we were still living in Florida. Toucan would come to the house and they would both get on my last nerve with their nonsense. They've even gone to a concert together. His fondness for Mike is what made it easy to share the negative stuff. He, like me, knew that Mike wasn't all bad. He was always saying, "Man, Mike's a good dude." and it was true. He would give me his honest opinion even when I didn't want to hear it. At the end of the day he believed I could do anything I set my mind to. He had a nonchalant, matter-of-fact attitude about everything I told him I wanted to do.

> **Me**: *I think I want to vacation on the moon.*
> **Toucan:** *Oh yeah? Well I'm sure you'll figure it out; you'll be alright.*

If I ever needed anything, be it money, a babysitter, someone to help us move 300 miles away, or someone to drive me to the hospital in the wee hours of the morning, I could count on Toucan. "Yes" first, questions and judgment later. He was also how I knew what was going on with everyone in the family, too. I didn't really need to reach out to them because he would give me updates. He kept in touch with everybody. I don't know how he managed it because there are a ton of us in this family.

He was the second cheerleader I ever recognized in my life. No doubt, others before him encouraged me and hoped the best for me, but he was second only to Mike in making me feel like I could accomplish any goal I set for myself.

My momma encouraged me, but for some reason momma's don't count. We expect them to cheer us on and when they do, they get no credit. Sad, but true. It's like this obligatory cheer. We tell ourselves they only cheer us on because they have to, not because it's true. It was different with Toucan. For one thing, he wasn't my momma, and another, he didn't believe in everybody so that made me special.

During one of our Saturday morning conversations, he told me was going to the hospital to have a cyst drained. He asked me to pray for him because he hated being in hospitals. This made me laugh a little, because he loved the medical field. He and his crazy momma and brother would watch these medical shows with real doctors and real surgeries. He also worked in the hospital and often considered going to nursing school. I guess it's one thing to give care and another to be on the receiving end. We talked for a little while more and I told him I would check in with him in a few days.

What started out as a routine procedure quickly turned into a nightmare. Toucan was admitted to the hospital to have a cyst drained, but turns out it wasn't a cyst. It was cancer. Due to complications of the procedure he wasn't able to leave the hospital right away. To make matters worse he somehow ended up with an infection, which complicated things further. I could feel time passing, the days were slipping away with all the energy focused on the complications, but what about the cancer? When would it get some attention?

I prayed for him all the time. I pleaded, I spoke in gentle soothing tones, I cried out in desperation. I went through so many phases of prayer. I did and said everything in my heart, requesting a healing and restoration for my cousin. There was no sign of improvement nor was there a clear plan of action, only one complication after the other. Let me say this, he was in Florida and I was in North Carolina which meant I didn't have all the details, but from where I was sitting nothing was being done to save his life.

Someone in the family suggested we fast and pray as a unit for him and believe God for his healing. I was all about it and this was the first time I managed to fast for longer than one meal. I cut out everything except fruits, veggies, nuts and water.

Every time there was a temptation I thought about what was on the line, literally life or death. I didn't even miss the meat after a few days. I continued to pray and make my request known to God.

I cried every single solitary day. It was nearly impossible to make it through the work day without needing to run to the bathroom. I cried everywhere, I even remember crying in my boss' office. I was a mess. I never stopped praying though and I never stopped believing. I was going home more often. Every time I had the opportunity to go home to Florida even just for a day I went. He was losing weight...so much weight. He didn't look like himself and even his voice changed. He was dying right before my eyes. I screamed and cried, my prayers no more than a little girl begging and pleading with God to change his mind begging him to choose a different course.

Please God, please God, oh God please save him.
Please don't do this to us.
I love him.
Is there not one righteous one among us God?
Not one can be found to plead on his behalf?

I couldn't breathe, my lungs struggled to do their job, while my heart worked overtime pumping so much so fast I felt as if my head would explode. Red hot tears ran down my face as I lay on the floor many days and many nights begging him to save Toucan. His situation wasn't getting better, things weren't improving, he continued to decline. My cries got louder...sobbing..weeping bitterly. My prayers changed again.

What kind of God sits back and does nothing?

What kind of God ignores the cries and prayers of his children?

You don't even care about him.

You don't even care about me.

My heart is heavy, God just give me rest.

I can't live like this. I don't want to live anymore.

Please God, please...oh God please!

Why aren't you listening? Don't you see he's dying? We all are...

January 5th, 2012 I received a strange call from my Auntie Hazel. I knew something was up...it was just weird.

> **Auntie Hazel:** *Hey, what y'all doing?*
> **Me:** *Nothing, the kids sitting in here on the computer.*
> **Auntie:** *Let me talk to Micah*
> **Micah:** *Hey "Baully".*
> **Micah:** *He's at work.*
> **Micah:** *He usually gets home around 4 or 5.*
> **Micah:** *Okay, love you too.*

What? She asked about Mike...she never asked about him like that before. I knew something was up and it was nothing good. I could feel it. Mike came home and immediately came in the house. This was out of the ordinary. For months he had been hanging outside with his friends until dark before even bothering to come inside. I knew no good would come from this.

I could hear him coming up the stairs, I went to the room not sure why, but I did. When he came into the bedroom I was facing the door as I stood at the foot of the bed with one hand on the foot board bracing myself. He had sad eyes as he approached me and closed the door behind him. I took one step back and started in:

> **Me:** *What's up Mike, why my Auntie calling here for you?*
>
> **Mike:** *Why don't you sit down?*
>
> **Me:** *uh no, say what you have to say.*
>
> **Mike:** *The doctors say there's nothing else they can do for him.*

Tears filled his eyes as he reached for me. I moved to avoid his touch

> **Me:** *SAY IT! You agreed to this, now say what you need to say.*

He paused for a moment and tried again.

> **Mike:** *There's just nothing these doctors can do for him, so they're sending him home, they're bringing in hospice to make him comfortable.*

My legs betrayed me, giving out under the weight of this news, as I fell to the floor he rushed to catch me. I held on to him crying, screaming, hitting him...attacking the messenger. He just held me. Until that moment, crying and hitting my husband with one hand and holding on for dear life with the other, I had never imagined that the reality of a slowly observed truth could still hit you so hard that it knocks the wind out of your lungs and the hope out of your heart. Like watching a train approach in slow motion you can see it for what it is, therefore you can anticipate it's arrival. I had watched this train approach for months, I had wished, hoped, and prayed it away in my mind yet here it was defying me and all the faith I had ever managed to hold onto. The reality of it standing in front of me big and bold in its ugliness demanding me to accept it and make peace with it's arrival left me shattered and broken and I knew only one thing for sure; there was no balm, no salve, no medicine or medicine man who could fix the brokenness of my soul, born out of this tragedy.

I knew my life would never be the same, my heart would never be whole and any semblance of joy was slowly slipping through my grasp just like he was. I couldn't hold on to him, but I didn't know how to let him go. I still don't.

A few days later, I went home to see him for his birthday. I didn't even recognize him as he lay in that bed. I lay on the floor of the room he was in, crying. He told me to get out if I was going to cry. I replied through my tears..."make me", I loved him. There wasn't anything I could do to change this. I had done all the praying I could and God refused to answer this prayer.

He had a complication that landed him back in the hospital and I went back to visit. I spent the night in the hospital. I didn't get any rest. He talked all night long. It was mostly nonsense. You know what I did then? I cried some more. My prayers didn't work, they didn't help...they had failed me.

I got the news during spring Break, my momma was in town with my nephews. My Auntie Hazel called her early that morning....Toucan was gone. I didn't cry, not right away anyway. Mike came to me and held me close, I breathed slowly..inhale, exhale. Then came the tears as I buried my face in his chest, it muffled the sounds of my sobbing. Once the crying stopped, I walked to the kitchen poured myself a sippy cup full of red wine. I bought the sippy cup a few months ago, it was a great way to drink wine in bed and not spill it.

> **Momma:** *Don't you think it's too early to drink.*
>
> **Me:** *Give a strong drink to him who is ready to perish and to those that be of heavy heart, Proverbs 31:6 God knows I need a drink right now Joyce.*

I turned and walked to my room, I could hear the darkness beckoning me to come to bed. "Darkness" is how my husband refers to my depression. "Don't give into the darkness." I could hear him saying as I closed the door behind me. I could feel the pull of the darkness and I had no desire to fight it. I wanted to drown in it, I took a few sips of the wine as I climbed into bed. I pulled the covers over my head to keep the sun out. I wanted my surroundings to match the darkness within. It was all over and there was nothing else that could be done. No going back, no miraculous healing, no hope...no resurrection.

The Funeral

There were so many people at my Auntie Hazel's house when I arrived. I didn't want to go in I wasn't sure if I could be in the room with people and talk about the fact that he was really gone. I didn't want to hear people sharing their favorite memories of him or whispering the same tired cliches when people pass away like, "he's in a better place," or "he's with the angels now." Like, shut up, you know what I mean? I was consumed by pain, grief and hopelessness. I wasn't there for a "pick me up", I was still trying to deal with his passing. Within a day or so of my arrival I found myself in a church full of people all dressed in red and black. The large church was almost filled to capacity with people standing along the walls as I was being ushered to a pew reserved for family. At the front of the church sat a pristine white casket with a hideous orange and green snapback sitting on top. He was a huge fan of University of Miami, our family was from Miami. I went to Florida State University, therefore, I bleed garnet and gold. It was something he often got on my last nerves about. If I hadn't been so overwhelmed with grief I would have chuckled a little at the sight of it.

Mike was by my side, holding my hand and holding me up. I was no more prepared for the gravesite than I was the church. I could not imagine that what I was feeling and seeing was reality. Consciously I knew it was actually happening, but my mind did not let me digest the full emotional weight of the moment. I'm sure this is some sort of psychological safety net to keep people on the right side of sanity. I was numb. I was emptied of emotion, reason and hope. All that remained was despair.

I'm not sure what is supposed to happen after a funeral. Are we expected to go back to our regularly scheduled program? I couldn't. After we returned home I refused to go back to my "normal" life. It was impossible. I just climbed into bed with sippy cup filled with wine and cried and drank.

Mike would come in the room and say "We need you." "You still have a family." "You can't die with Toucan." "We love you." I didn't want to hear any of that. I just wanted to die. I started praying again.

God please take me out of this world, this pain is more than I can bear.

God keep my children safe as you let me die in my sleep.

God why do you refuse to let me die? I can't do this anymore.

I don't want to live anymore, Lord can you at least let me die in my sleep?

Lord don't let my kids find me in the morning.

After awhile I realized what I was saying. I was willing to leave my kids without a mother. I prayed more.

God my kids would be better off without me.

What kind of mother begs to die knowing she has children?

I am a horrible mother God and my kids deserve better, please just let me die.

Mike deserves a better wife than me God, just let me die and help him find a woman that would be good for him and my kids.

I didn't want to move on, I didn't want to get better. I felt like to do so would be saying I was okay with Toucan's passing. I would NEVER say that. Never. There was no moving on. I went back to work, I went through the motions of living, but when my work day was over it was back to my bedroom, in the dark with my tears and my wine until the next day.

The weight of the grief and sorrow was heavy, it was definitely more than I could bear. I simply could not get up from under the weight of it all. To make matters worse, my grief lead to full-blown depression. It hurt to get up and move through the day, every sad thought about Toucan led me down a rabbit-hole so deep and dark that there was no light to be found. As I lay at the bottom of the hole, it was cold, damp and distant from any happiness, or hope of it in the future.

Things would never get better. How could they? Toucan wasn't coming back and there was no denying that harsh reality. I didn't have the energy or even the desire to work on my marriage. I was so consumed by the darkness that it was impossible for me to be involved with my kids. I don't know what they were doing during this time. I don't know how they managed. I just kept the same routine of faking it during the day, crying and drinking at night. If I wasn't in my room in my bed under the covers with my sippy cup filled with wine, I wanted to be.

The darkness called out to me, it drew me in. Oddly, there was some peace about it. I started to look forward to it. I was alone, I didn't have to pretend like I was over Toucan's passing, I didn't have to take care of anything or anyone, no need for conversation or explaining what or how I was feeling, just cold...silent....darkness. I often thought about dying. Fantasized is probably more accurate. After spending so much time in the darkness, preferring it to real life, death seemed like a prize.

> *What if I could just go to sleep and never get up? It would all be over. I was married to a man who loved me, but was no longer "in love" with me and that for me was the real deal breaker. I had kids who deserved a better mother than I had been. I was a drain on my friends, who would also be better off without me to worry about.*

I felt like if I didn't end my own life then certainly the suffering would take on a persona and kill me. I was never bothered by that idea, I would welcome death in any way, shape, or form that it might manifest. The grief and hopelessness outweighed every perceivable "good" thing I had in my life. It was like a huge lead blanket, suffocating and holding me down.

That's the thing with depression, your mind is so messed up no matter what your reality is you can't see it. You can't feel the love people have for you, you can only see and feel the pain. You can't imagine things will get any better and the thought of living a life in that type of darkness is more than you can bear. Suicide starts to look like a pretty good option. Not only an option, but relief. Depression for me was like an emotional and mental pain from which there was never any relief. It left me feeling completely alone in the world and like everyone I was connected to would be better off without me.

CHAPTER EIGHT

Sunshine And Rain

Death did not come and I never had the strength to take my own life. I was just living in darkness. I was exhausted. My husband, my friends and my family never stopped trying to reach me and encourage me to get back to living. They all believed it was possible for me even if I didn't.

The summer after Toucan's passing was pretty uneventful, but I was trying to be better. It wasn't working, I was still sad, but I tried. I was going to church and the music and sermons were really good. I felt this shift while I was there, it was a momentary lifting of the weight I continued to carry, but it didn't last past the parking lot. I was working at Carmel Christian as the elementary Spanish teacher. I thought I would get the same feeling being at work, but I didn't. Aside from a few people I was friendly with, I didn't feel like I "belonged" there. That did not help with the depression. I loved the kids, as a teacher you always love the kids, it's everyone else you have a problem with.

One of my favorite people, was a lady named Pam. Pam was the music teacher. We couldn't have been more different on the outside, but we are basically the same person on the inside. She is funny, sassy, no nonsense and sarcastic. I loved her immediately. I thought she was crazy...I was right and I loved her even more. Pam was on weight watchers and she had lost a lot of weight. I was inspired to start up again too. We would spend our breaks together, walking on the track, disrupting classrooms with our shenanigans and laughing through all of it. She spoke highly of me to staff members that had not treated me kindly. It makes me smile now just thinking about some of the shade she threw in a staff meeting once.

She wanted to come to my church because she loved great gospel choirs. We set a date and she showed up. The music was great, but we had a guest speaker and he was white. She leaned over and whispered "so you invited me on the day the white guys preaching? Shame on you." We giggled and enjoyed the sermon.

She then started inviting me to her church. She went to Elevation. If you live in Charlotte and you haven't heard of Elevation Church you must live under a rock. I was fine to visit Elevation, but that would mean I would miss my own pastor and I needed that pick-me-up each week, even if it was only for a few hours. As God would have it, my pastor when on sabbatical. We were left with guest preachers and I was fine with missing one of them. I agreed to attend Elevation with her, so we set a date.

I don't live under a rock so I had heard of Elevation. It was a "white" church and many sites from my Google search called it a cult. I, however, trusted Pam. If it were a cult, she definitely would not be attending and if she did she wouldn't be crazy enough to invite me.

I pulled into the parking lot, just a few minutes later than Pam had suggested. I could not believe my eyes. There was a line as far as the eyes could see. It reminded me of the lines at Disney World, that wound back and forth so the line was actually longer than it appeared. Insane! I called her and she waved to me from somewhere in the middle of the line. I joined her and asked if it was like that every week. She said yes.

As we waited in line there were people walking around in gray shirts, holding orange folders and smiling like they had just won the lottery, or like they were on drugs. This lady walked by asking if there were any "first time visitors" and before I could tell Pam to keep her mouth shut she had already raised her hand to identify me as a first time guest. I didn't even smile at the lady. I was thinking,

> *Why is she standing so close to me?*
> *Why is she smiling so damn hard?*
> *How can I get rid of her?*
> *What? She walking with us?*

97

Yeah this might be a cult and she has clearly been drinking the koolaide.

I wish I could say once we were inside things improved. They did not. The music was so loud you could hear it in the lobby area. It was like house music..or club music, but definitely not church music not even for white people. I didn't know what kinda church this was.

We found our seats and the worship music started. It wasn't like the music they were playing as we entered, but it wasn't like music I had heard before either. I grew up in a black church listening to gospel music. Even when I attended a white church the music was not like what they were playing at Elevation. It was actually good and yes I say "actually" because I was surprised I was enjoying it. Then this little dude takes the stage. He was dressed like white guys dress who have black friends. He was not dressed like a pastor, he didn't look like one either.

I will never forget that sermon. It was during the "Expectation Gap" series. His sermon topic was When God Doesn't Meet Your Expectations. I was like YEP, let's talk about that right there. He preached from the story of Lazarus. Lazarus was Mary's brother and he was friends with Jesus. He got sick and they sent word to Jesus, upon hearing the news that Lazarus was sick Jesus, didn't rush to the side of his closest friend, nope he took his precious time and waited a few days before making the trip. Jesus said "this sickness will not be unto death." I knew this story very well. It was the one I used and prayed when I first heard the news of Toucan's cancer. I proclaimed aloud as I cried out to God "this sickness will not be unto death."

Pastor Steven continued, When Jesus finally arrived Mary ran out to the gate to meet Jesus. She was not happy with him. He retold this section with much attitude and his hand on his hip. It's exactly how I felt when Jesus had not shown up for me. Mary tells Jesus, oh, now you wanna come and see about Lazarus? Y'all was supposed to be boys too, if you had come earlier he wouldn't be dead right now. I'm paraphrasing as Pastor Steven did that day.

Then he said something that made me sit up and gather my things. He said "sometimes this life with God can be disappointing." "AMEN!!" I thought, you are right about that. I expected him to follow it up with a, but "it all works out in the end" type of statement, but he didn't. He said it again. "Sometimes this life with God can be disappointing." Then he just stood there.

He didn't clean it up, he just continued to say it doesn't always work out the way we hope and sometimes the marriage does end and you do lose the job. I thought, or you do bury your cousin.

He finished his sermon by saying he didn't want to present a life with Christ as if it was one without any heartaches or disappointments. He didn't want to set us up for that type of failure. He wanted us to know sometimes we would be disappointed and hurt, but even if that were true God was still good. Bad situation, good God. It was the first time I saw a true glimmer of hope. The way things ended with Toucan would ALWAYS suck, BUT God was still good. I didn't accept it, but I was willing to consider it as a real possibility.

I left church that day so thankful for Pam and completely intrigued by Pastor Steven and Elevation church. I knew I would return. I took my children with me the following week. They LOVED it and immediately signed up to volunteer. I was much more reluctant, but I was glad we had found a place we could attend together.

I believe being surrounded by other believers and getting a good word from Pastor Steven each week is what made the difference. It began to chip away at whatever was keeping me from breaking free from the depression. I wasn't quite able to take hold of it for myself, but I had faith things could get better for me. I hadn't experienced it, but I knew other people who had overcome their struggle with depression and I thought if they could do it so could I.

But, those hopeful possibilities sent me into another cycle of depression. How could I betray Toucan by being happy after his passing? My grief and depression were welded together.

Every time I was sad about Toucan, I was reminded of my selfish desire to get past it. This was the quickest route down yet another rabbit hole. I felt shame as my desire to be happy and emotionally stable made me question my loyalty and love for Toucan. If my life got better, I felt like I had benefited from his death, it was like saying I was okay with him dying and I would NEVER say that.

And there was still my marriage. On top of my internal conflict about moving past grieving and wanting to be happy, I was also struggling with embarrassment of feeling weak and lonely. I longed for a relationship with my husband who seemed perfectly content with the way things were between us. He didn't want to see me depressed, he just wanted me "back to normal." It wasn't getting better it just wasn't as bad.

The house was quieter because we didn't yell as much. I still felt unloved, uncherished and like I was his biggest mistake. I felt as though he regretted being married to me, but he was determined to stay for our children. He is so loyal and big on family, unfortunately that is not enough for me. I wanted and desperately needed him to be big on me. Even with everything we had been through I still wanted our marriage to work. I didn't really believe it was possible though. I wasn't asking (or believing) for great things in our marriage, just that we wouldn't fight and we could quietly live separate lives under the same roof until our children graduated from high school. Once the kids were out of the house we could divorce, he wouldn't have a reason to stay.

I still loved him though. I wanted to believe we could have a good marriage. Throughout the history of our relationship we had seasons when things were good followed by seasons of fighting and threatening divorce. We were never consistent. Whenever I read something in the bible or a bible study book on how a wife should be treated I would think to myself "Is that even possible for us?" I would read devotionals or watch movies about marriage and would think.."He should be watching this so he could learn a thing or two about how I deserve to be treated."

In my mind I was already treating him with love and respect and he was getting the better deal because I was giving him everything, but getting nothing in return. He always withheld love and affection by keeping me at distance because he wanted out, but he didn't want to be the one to leave, at least that's how I saw it.

My situations and circumstances were unchanging. My heart was heavy with grief for Toucan and I longed to be loved by my husband. I was still experiencing horrible grief and crying myself to sleep as I thought about my marriage and my life. There finally came a day where I had the courage to admit to myself that I wanted better and that better was a real possibility.

I continued to attend Elevation and I began to pray more and study my bible. I felt no change at all, but I was committed to keeping the faith even when it didn't feel like things would ever get better. Believing in something again made a difference even if I couldn't feel it right away. I continued to battle depression and self doubt. There was a darkness inside me, spreading negative thoughts and negative self-talk. I was still going to church not "faking it," but expecting for something to change in me. It didn't. My marriage wasn't improving either even though I had started to implement strategies and changes from my studies in the word of God. There was still an ocean between us and not a boat or a bridge in sight.

While going through it I couldn't see any change at all, but looking back I realize what I had overlooked. I actually was changing. Not in the ways I'd hoped or even in ways that were noticeable to me then, but I was changing nonetheless. It was my faith. I had gotten a hold of it, or it had gotten a hold of me and I was committed to staying the course until something changed. I had faith in God. I believed he existed and I believed he was good even though I'd been through some difficult things in my life. I believed God ordained marriage and would save mine if I let him. I believed my life could get better if I let God in to clean up the mess I had made. I had a new found faith after re-dedicating my life to Christ.

Power
of
Identity

CHAPTER NINE

Power Principle #1

"You Are Who God Says You Are"

We are created by God. If we are to unfold and discover our true identity we must go to the Creator. How can we, the created, determine who we are and the purpose of our lives? I'd like to help you discover your true identity based on who God says you are.

I now understand who God says I am, but before I truly understood that, I struggled with who I thought I was. Self-identity can be complicated. How we identify ourselves is based on a number of factors. It begins with the labels we give ourselves, "black," "white," "man," "woman" and how we feel about those labels, "smart," "dumb," "ugly," "beautiful" and then expands to include how society feels about those labels as well, "strong," "weak," "successful."

Unfortunately, the process of self-identity begins when we are children, but is influenced one-hundred percent by our environment and those in it. We are taught who we are and the limitations or expectations based on that identity before we even have the opportunity to discover ourselves. Our parents, teachers and the world around us tell us that girls wear pink and play with dolls and boys wear blue and play with trucks. If for some odd reason we go against those "truths" we are quickly corrected.

As you get older, however, you begin to take more ownership in the self identification process. You may start to form your identity based on your experiences, how you see the world and the decisions you've made. If you've made "good" decisions based on whatever value system you use, then you are a "good" person and you believe you are entitled to good things. On the other hand, if you've made some bad decisions or a few mistakes and have suffered the consequences, you probably feel you are a "bad" person and deserve all the bad things coming your way. You don't deserve good in your life because good isn't for a person like you.

Even worse yet is defining your identity based on how others have treated you. If you were mistreated and abused or neglected you use it to form your identity. Your thought system is in alignment with the pain and hurt you've experienced. You are "unworthy" because if you had value people would treat you better. We don't know who we truly are, so we behave according to the labels we have accepted or those handed to us by others. It's no wonder many of us are suffering from confusion, anxiety, frustration and depression caused by this "identity crisis".

Take a moment to think about your own labels. What "truths" have you accepted about your identity? Do people like you go to college, start businesses, or travel the world? Is the expectation for you to get a good job with benefits and to avoid risks? How are you expected to behave, how should you expect to be treated by others? Are people like you smart enough, cool enough or special enough?

At my lowest point, I believed I was just a girl who got pregnant in high school, by some guy I wasn't even in a relationship with and was so pathetic I had been cheated on twice by the man I trapped by having kids. As you can see, self-identification and self-identity is definitely a flawed system. When you adhere to the rules of this system, your identity changes based on your circumstances, your experiences and an ever-changing societal view. You could never be more than your circumstance and with no control over the past you could never amount to more than the sum of your mistakes. I identified broken, flawed, unworthy and unloved. The more I attended church and studied my bible I begin to realize something: God had a completely different identity for me than I had for myself. I needed to discover and accept who I truly was because I would never grow beyond the characteristics and abilities of the identity I thought was mine. God has a lot to say about who we are:

You are a child of God.

"Wherefore thou art no more a servant, but a son; and if a son, then an heir of God through Christ."
~Galatians 4:7 KJV

When I was living my life and dealing with my grief and depression, dealing with the state of my marriage, I thought I knew how to handle it. I thought I knew what I needed and how things "worked." Once I accepted the fact that I was a child, God's child, I realized I knew nothing. Less than nothing. All I thought I knew had gotten me to where I was and I wasn't thrilled about my life. If my best thinking and navigating the world couldn't produce any better quality fruit, I might need some help. It made me open to asking, seeking and following God in every area of my life.

Depending on your natural experience in the child-parent relationship the fact that you are a child of God can either bring you peace or anxiety. My childhood was so lit! I had parents who loved and took care of me. They provided for me and encouraged me. My mother always gave me the best wisdom and guidance she could and my dad did the best he could too. The truth is though, they were both limited by their own experiences, knowledge and resources.

Maybe you didn't have parents who took care of you. Perhaps the very people who were supposed to protect and love you allowed you to be abused and neglected. There is no excuse for the pain and hurt they caused. You have to understand though the reason for that hurt and pain wasn't because of their role as your parent or because of your role as their child, but it was born out of their brokenness.

If you are a parent, you can look back over the years of your parenting and see where you did the best you could with what you had, but also acknowledge it was less than your child deserved. Whether it's because you didn't know, you didn't care or simply didn't have what you needed to do better, you messed up. That's okay. The good news is this child-parent relationship between you and God will not fall prey to the same shortcomings of your natural relationship. God is not operating from a broken place. He is not limited in resources, knowledge, love or anything else for that matter.

You are chosen, royal, holy and God's special possession.

"*But you are a chosen people, a royal priesthood, a holy nation, God's special possession, that you may declare the praises of him who called you out of the dark into his wonderful light.*"
~*1 Peter 2:9 NIV*

You **are** chosen, not "you were chosen before you made all those mistakes and those people mistreated you." Nope. You ARE chosen right now, even though you've run from the calling, even with all the mistakes you've made and how hurt you've been. You are God's chosen one. It's one thing to be chosen by someone who doesn't know you and doesn't know the darkness of your past...or your present. But to know and see all the ugly bits of your life and still be chosen, brings a certain amount of peace and freedom to your heart. You don't have to hide or pretend with God, he knows all and sees all and still chooses you.

God calls you "royal" and "holy." Granted these may be a little more difficult to accept, but it doesn't make them any less true. Imagine you were born to the king and queen of a great nation. Your family lineage makes you royal. You were born into it. You didn't earn it and you didn't necessarily "deserve" it, but you are royalty nonetheless. Whether or not you experience life as royalty depends on whether or not you accept this truth. Will you live your life in a way that reflects your true identity? When you understand who you are and accept the family line you belong to, you will accept nothing less. You will expect respect from others and will carry yourself in a way that is becoming of the kingdom you represent.

You **are** holy. When you accept the fact that you are holy you realize it's not something you have to earn. It's a good thing too because who could ever earn "holiness"? With the number of mistakes we make in a day, we might last all of five minutes before our "holy" status is quickly taken away from us. You can choose to live holy because you are holy or you can make the decision to behave in a manner which doesn't honor who you truly are. You can't choose to be holy, you are holy, but you can decide whether or not you will live it out.

Not only are you chosen, royal and holy, but God calls you his *special possession*. Have you ever had something that was very special to you, something of high value, something that couldn't be replaced? How did you treat your special possession? You probably took great care of it and even showed it off to friends and family. You may have even put it in a place where it could be protected and safe from accidental damage. You probably spend time using it, or admiring it depending on how you get the most enjoyment from it.

You are more than some fancy thing to God. You are his special possession. He purchased you at a high cost. He sent his son Jesus to die for you and redeemed you from the enemy. He wants to use you for the purpose for which you were created.

If you are who God says you are then you are his child, chosen, royal, holy and his special possession. It is clear that your true identity is not only found in the word of God, but it is found in God himself. It is impossible to define yourself and get a real understanding of who you are outside of or separate from the one who called you into existence. To get a full understanding, we have to go beyond our identity and take a look at the identity of God.

CHAPTER TEN

God Is...

There are not enough words to aptly describe the fullness of God. I will attempt to give you an idea of who he is. Please understand that while I have a way with words, there are not enough words known to man to fully describe and identify God.

God is the Creator.

"For by him were all things created, that are in heaven, and that are in earth, visible and invisible, whether they be thrones, or dominions, or principalities, or powers: all things were created by him, and for him." Colossians 1:16

Every single thing that we see was created by God. He did this without any input, he started with no raw materials, he didn't have a blueprint and he didn't have an instruction manual. He literally spoke things into existence. "Let there be light.", and light existed. By his word nations rise and fall, life, death, health and healing all bend and bow to his will and his word. His creative power knows no end. As I look out my window I see trees and grass in my front yard, shrubs and flowers in my neighbors yard. Those things exist, I can see them, touch them and smell them because of God's words.

He created the life cycle of nature with his words commanding the trees to come forth and to produce seeds that would produce more trees of their own kind. Seasons change, winds blow carrying with them potential for new life, seeds are planted, rain falls and new life springs forth from the ground. It's easy to forget or dismiss his creative power because we become accustomed to our surroundings. Everything we see regularly becomes commonplace.

I remember one year Mike and I went to Boston for our anniversary and to visit family. Our anniversary is in March, which is still snow season in New England. In case you don't remember, I am a Florida girl. I grew up with winters reaching an arctic 30 degrees at the height of winter. It wasn't uncommon for people to go to the beach during Christmas Break. I had never seen snow before.

Needless to say, when we arrived by plane to Boston I began screaming on the plane, "Oh my goodness, oh my goodness, can you see that down there? Can you see the snow? Oh my goodness it's just like on tv, perfect little squares of snow." Once we touched down and walked to the car, my excitement did not let up. As the weight of my foot crushed the snow I let out squeals of joy. No one else was amused by me or the snow. My brother-in-law looked at my husband as if to suggest I needed a mental check-up.

My husband is from New York, as is his brother. They saw snow every winter, so they did not share in my enthusiasm. I, however, was in amazement. I felt like God was so amazing. I had a great appreciation for his handiwork. I could see God in the snow. I was, however, blind to his awesomeness and handiwork as I stared out at the beach when I was growing up. It was commonplace to me so I was not excited by the beach. I don't get why people are so excited by it. The sand is horrible, the salt, the crowds...ugh.

If you are reading this book from the comfort of your home located in a state that is completed landlocked and you would give your right eye to stare out at the beach whenever you want, you probably don't understand me and would like to smack me right now. How can I not see how amazing God is when looking at the beach? Easy. I grew up less than 15-minutes driving distance from the beach and about a 45-minute walk for my entire life. Not that exciting. When we see it everyday, we can forget we are looking at the work of God's word.

We even discount the incredible creation and reproduction of our own species. Births seem to be so commonplace and with the advances in medicine, pregnancies don't always cause us to stop and admire the creative power of God. Yes we like babies, most of us anyway, but we are excited because they are "cute" and "small" and "smell nice"...like a puppy.

I wonder how often we think of the perfect steps that have to be in place for a woman to carry a child inside her own body and then literally give birth to new life. When I think about the science of it all and everything that could and does go wrong during conception, gestation and delivery, it is truly a testament to the power of our Creator when new life springs forth.

Even things that we now call man-made could not exist if it weren't for God. Who provided the materials? Where did the revelation, inspiration or vision come from? God gives man the ability, skills and knowledge needed to create. All of the advances in technology, medicine and every other industry started with God and by God. His creative power, however, does not stop at the physical world. He can also speak a word to create opportunities, solutions and protection. He can resurrect marriages with one word, bringing forth life in a relationship you previously thought was dead. There is truly no limit to his creative power.

God is a Way Maker

" **16** Thus saith the Lord, which maketh a way in the sea, and a path in the mighty waters;

17 Which bringeth forth the chariot and horse, the army and the power; they shall lie down together, they shall not rise: they are extinct, they are quenched as tow.

18 Remember ye not the former things, neither consider the things of old.

19 Behold, I will do a new thing; now it shall spring forth; shall ye not know it? I will even make a way in the wilderness, and rivers in the desert."~ Isaiah 43:16-19 KJV

God will make a way, emphasis on the word "make." The bible is not saying he will find or discover a way. It's saying he will create a way where none exists. The story of Moses crossing the Red sea is a perfect example of this. The children of Israel, being led by Moses, left Egypt toward the land God promised them. As they journeyed to the promised land the Egyptian soldiers began to pursue them. They reached the Red Sea and could see no way to escape being captured by the soldiers who were fast approaching. The sea was wide, deep and impossible to swim or cross without a bridge or boat in sight.

I'm not sure what the Israelites were thinking, but I would have been afraid facing such a hopeless situation. Can you imagine the mothers trying to console their children who were old enough to understand what was happening? How helpless they must have felt, having a desire to save their children, but not having the power to do so. The men must have felt the same way, seeing their families in such a horrible predicament but unable to protect them. I can imagine friends embracing one another in an attempt to console each other and to prepare for the worst.

How completely mind-blowing it must have been to see God move and make a way through the Red Sea! Moses lifting his hand, stretching out his staff in faith and the water beginning to part.The Israelites and all they had with them, crossed the Red Sea on dry land. After they made it across, the Egyptian soldiers continued in pursuit, but as the Red Sea came crashing down on them, found their graves at the bottom of the sea never to be seen again. God made a way where none existed. This is the incredible event mentioned in the scripture above. God is a way-maker. It sets the stage for the real question: "Don't you see God is doing a new thing? Simply put, he did it before and he will do it again by any means necessary.

I want you to know that no matter what your situation looks like God will make a way for you. Don't get stuck on how he did it before, he will make a way out of no way, even if he has to create a new plan to do it. We can find ourselves in situations similar to ones we've been confronted with in the past. If God doesn't show up the way he did before we doubt that he will at all. But God's way-making skills are not limited by our ability to see him at work. Sometimes we believe it's over because we can't "see" how God is working to get us out of our predicament. God's power is not diminished just because we don't see him.

Maybe you're wondering what God's power has to do with you. You're in a relationship with God, right? You're his kid, he chose you and you are his special possession. Consider your own parents for a moment. Regardless of their desire, they are limited in what they're able to do for you. They can't love you if they don't love themselves. They can't forgive you for what you've done in the past if they can't forgive themselves. The opportunities they provide you with are also limited to their resources, their circle of influence and their desire to help. They certainly can't heal you when you're sick, or help you cross the Red Sea on dry land. Your earthly parents have limited power.

God does not face those limitations. He is the creator of the parent-child relationship and there is no limit to what he can and will do for you. No matter what you are up against you have a Father in Heaven whose power and ability are limitless. Even when you don't know what you need, when the door seems not only closed, but locked it is no match for God. He will not hesitate to act on your behalf.

Look, I don't know you, but certainly you might be a friend or a relative who has purchased this book to support me. I appreciate it too. I hope you know that if there was something I could do for you I would do it, I would totally return the favor. I don't even have to really like someone to do something for them, especially if it's easy to do. How many times in your life have you held the door open for someone, or let them cut in line? Maybe you opened your home to a family member or friend in need. So nice of you. As nice as we can be, we pale in comparison to God, of course. This isn't a competition, and it's a good thing because, if it were we would definitely lose.

My point is, if we... who are flawed, sinful, emotionally unstable, and are restricted by time, space and resources, would lend a helping hand, why wouldn't God do the same for you? The answer is, he absolutely would. YOU'RE HIS KID! HE IS THE FATHER!

I won't pretend that all fathers do what they are able or even what they should for their kids. There are relatives all over this world not willing to cross the street to help out their family members. You may be related to individuals like this, so you think just because you and God have a relationship, it doesn't guarantee anything. It's possible your past is full of friends and family that were supposed to help, but instead they hurt or watched you struggle.

First of all, God is not a man and is not controlled by flesh or a sinful nature. Second, you're not the child he wish he never had or a friend he's jealous of. No, YOU are the object of his affection. He loves you. More than that... God IS love.

God is love

7 Beloved, let us love one another: for love is of God; and every one that loveth is born of God, and knoweth God.
8 He that loveth not knoweth not God; for God is love.

9 In this was manifested the love of God toward us, because that God sent his only begotten Son into the world, that we might live through him.

10 Herein is love, not that we loved God, but that he loved us, and sent his Son to be the propitiation for our sins.

When you read the statement "God is love", what does that mean to you? How do you define love? I wonder if we even know what the word "love" means. It is often used to describe how we feel about everything from our loved ones to our favorite dish and even those cute little alpacas pics on instagram. [I LOVE alpacas!! So cute.] You'd think the more we use it the more we would recognize it when we see it. The problem [with love] is that we have widespread use of the word, but apply it sparingly in its purest form. Love, however, originated in God and so in order to really understand what love is we have to follow the Creator's definition.

1 Corinthians 13:4-7 (NIV)

4 Love is patient, love is kind. It does not envy, it does not boast, it is not proud.

5 It does not dishonor others, it is not self-seeking, it is not easily angered, it keeps no record of wrongs.

6 Love does not delight in evil but rejoices with the truth.

7 It always protects, always trusts, always hopes, always perseveres.

God's definition of love is quite the tall order. Let's take it step by step.

Love is patient.

As I'm writing this book I'm trying to think of a situation where being patient is easy. I wanted to start this section off by saying "being patient is easy when ....", but I couldn't think of an example. I don't know of a time when being patient has been easy for me or anyone else. Some, people are naturally patient. They wait and they are comfortable with waiting, but for the rest of us...we will wait...if we HAVE to. Being patient is showing capacity for endurance . Our reality is we all wait, we don't have a choice. Waiting doesn't necessarily mean you are being patient. Being patient isn't just waiting, it's about enduring quietly, without complaint. Love is being able to wait well for as long as you need, without complaint, irritation or frustration.

Love is kind.

Being kind, in my opinion, is easier than being patient. It gets easier the more you extend kindness to people you like, people you love or people you think deserve some small token of kindness. Simply, "not being mean", does not constitute being kind. While silence might be the kindest thing you can do when that relative reminds you how much weight you've gained, or wonders when you will finally get married, that doesn't really count. Kindness requires more than refraining from gossip, clapbacks, throwing shade or crass behavior. It requires action in a positive direction. Love is speaking a word of encouragement or doing something in service for someone else's benefit.

It does not envy, it does not boast, it is not proud.

Envy is the fruit of pride and ego, it's also a lack of trust. It is not, however, an act of love. When we are envious we are jealous about someone else's opportunities, life, personal relationships, or finances. We feel they don't deserve them or haven't worked hard enough. We believe we are more deserving than they are and see this as "unfair". Love does not behave this way. Love allows us to be happy for the "wins" of others. Envy also reveals a lack of trust in God's divine timing and distribution of blessings. God is the giver of blessings and he does so in his timing. Envy says. "We want what they've been blessed with and we want it now."

The spirit of boasting and pride, on the other hand, aims at robbing God of the glory due him. We mistakenly behave as if our achievements are of our own doing. We boast because we think we are better than those who don't share our accomplishments or haven't achieved at the same level. We must remember God is the giver of all and provides everything, including our very breath. Boasting and pride aren't born of love for God or for those around us. It's love of self.

It does not dishonor others, it is not self-seeking, it is not easily angered, it keeps no record of wrongs.

What does it even mean to honor another person? I think it's not only how we treat and speak to them, but also how we speak about them. Are we exposing their flaws and shortcomings to others for validation, justification of our behaviors, comic relief or just to fill the silence? Either way, it is dishonoring even if it is becoming a social norm. We want to get our way and get our needs met first and when we don't, we respond negatively and want people to understand "where we are coming from."

I used to dishonor my husband when we were fighting. I wanted to tell my friends or family how horrible he was, because I wanted them to understand my bad behavior. If I'm honest, it was a cycle. Because I was self-seeking, wanting my needs met first, if he didn't comply, I was quick to anger, kept great records and dishonored him in my actions and words. Not because I didn't love him, but because I didn't know how to love him. I didn't understand what love really was. We are all naturally selfish. We want what we want and society says that's okay. We have a right to what we want and we can act out when we don't get it. Maybe it's the norm, but it's not love.

Love honors others, seeks to serve, assumes the best, forgives quickly and forgets wrongdoings.

Love does not delight in evil but rejoices with the truth.

Taking joy in someone else's pain or someone else's downfall is not love. Even when they brought it on themselves, maybe they ignored warnings or advice, but it still doesn't make it right. Love does not find pleasure in someone else's pain. When we want to get revenge or give them what they "deserve" we are truly delighting in evil. There was a time where I would say things to hurt my husband because I had been hurt by him. Real love rejoices with the truth. It's not always easy to hear or face, but the truth always takes us closer to God.

It always protects, always trusts, always hopes, always perseveres.

Love protects us from physical and emotional harm, whether the threat is internal or external. When my kids were small I would have to take things from them, keep them out of the kitchen and sometimes literally restrain them in order to protect them. They didn't understand it most of the time and definitely didn't enjoy it, but I protected them because I love them. The idea that love always trusts is very difficult because once you've been hurt before, it doesn't seem like a smart strategy. I mean, "fool me once shame on me"...right? Not so with love. It isn't about trusting in people though. It's not suggesting that you trust in a person who has continuously hurt you. Love is about trusting in the process, trusting in God. I think the last two go hand in hand. If you always hope then you will persevere. I see perseverance as a determination not to quit or slow down in your efforts and therefore a favorable outcome is inevitable.

I have great friends and a great family, but I don't know one person on this planet who has ever showed me the kind of love described here. I know for a fact I have never loved anyone that way. Not my children, not my husband, not even myself. It seems like an impossible task. Who could possibly love like this? God, that's who. He IS Love. You can replace the word love with "God" to get a better understanding of who God is.

> *God is patient, God is kind. He does not envy, He does not boast, He is not proud. He does not dishonor others, he is not self-seeking, he is not easily angered, he keeps no record of wrongs. God does not delight in evil but rejoices with the truth. He always protects, always trusts, always hopes, always perseveres.*

It's not that he has love for you, but he IS love. His very nature, the substance of his character is LOVE. Maybe you have never experienced this type of love in relationships with your parents or relatives or even your spouse, but this is who God is and who he will be in your life if you allow him.

CHAPTER ELEVEN

Your Purpose

There is power in your identity. Knowing who you are, is essential in transforming your life. You don't have to continue through life just doing "whatever." You were created to be who you are because God has a purpose for you. Your purpose is not about living a "spoiled" life or getting what you want all the time. It's about more than that.

Good Works

8 For by grace are ye saved through faith; and that not of yourselves: it is the gift of God:
9 Not of works, lest any man should boast.
10 For we are his workmanship, created in Christ Jesus unto good works, which God hath before ordained that we should walk in them.
~ Ephesians 2:8-10 KJV

Many times in the christian circle salvation is presented as if it is the end goal. We have this attitude, "I'm not going to hell, whew, now I can just put my feet up and wait for Jesus to return." Uh, no. You were saved through Jesus Christ so you could do good works. These "good works" have been prepared by God with you in mind.

Salvation is not about you just sitting back enjoying the "good life." You are meant to have an impact, you are called to serve others. What you do isn't as important as why and how you do it. We must ask ourselves am I adding value to people and am I doing it in a manner which will bring honor and glory to the God I serve?

Once we identify with who we are and who God has called us to be then we realize we have work to do. I realize we don't always know where to start. "Okay Courage, my Father is dope and I have a purpose...now what?" You have to start with what you have. God has equipped you with what you need to get the job done. You just have to take a good look at yourself and take inventory of your gifts and talents as you begin this journey.

And yes, you definitely have gifts and talents even if you can't think of what they are right now. Yes, I'm sure.

Through Your Gifts And Talents

> **10** As every man hath received the gift, even so minister the same one to another, as good stewards of the manifold grace of God.
> **11** If any man speak, let him speak as the oracles of God; if any man minister, let him do it as of the ability which God giveth: that God in all things may be glorified through Jesus Christ, to whom be praise and dominion for ever and ever. Amen.
> ~1 Peter 4:10-11 KJV

Every man, woman and child has been given a gift by God and we are to use those gifts and talents to serve one another. Don't be wasteful. If you have the gift of speaking, then speak, gift to teach, then teach. Whatever your gift, do it with the respect it deserves. Understand it is a gift from God so he would be glorified. You have a gift. You may have difficulty recognizing it or you may not see it as a gift at all, but according to scripture every person has been given a gift and that includes you. You are gifted and talented in some area.

When we feel we don't have gifts or when we are unable to recognize the gifts we have it can lead to feelings of unworthiness or make us believe we have no value. We can also begin to feel like failures, especially if we have already arrived at a place where we feel the pull towards a greater purpose for our lives. Pray about it, ask God to reveal the true nature of your gifts and talents. Begin to think on things you find easy and enjoyable.

Another thing I suggest is talking to trusted friends and family. Simply ask them what they think your gifts are and why. You have to be careful here though. It must be someone one you can trust, someone who knows there's a greater purpose for their life as well. When our gifts don't look like everyone else's or don't seem important it can be even more difficult to discover.

Varied Gifts

3 And I have filled him with the spirit of God, in wisdom, and in understanding, and in knowledge, and in all manner of workmanship,
4 To devise cunning works, to work in gold, and in silver, and in brass,
5 And in cutting of stones, to set them, and in carving of timber, to work in all manner of workmanship.
~ Exodus 31:3-5 KJV

I remember when I started thinking about my gifts. I had a very difficult time. I thought of things I enjoyed doing. Singing. I love singing. I know it's not my gift because I sound horrible. I am not artistic, I can't build anything. I'm a pretty good cook, but I do it out of necessity and because I love to eat. All I could think of were gifts I didn't have or things I didn't do well.

This is not at all helpful. I was looking for certain types of gifts. I think what made it even more challenging is that I was looking at it from an entrepreneurial standpoint. I had an overwhelming desire to start my own business. I was not interested in a gift that could be used in the church either. I didn't want to preach, I can't sing and I wasn't qualified to teach. All of this pretty much left me with nothing.

Once I realized my gift was speaking and teaching, I quickly wished I had different gifts. Why couldn't I be a singer or a dancer, that would be so much more fun? I wished I had a more tangible gift like my friends Olivia and Quia. You can easily see their gifts. They are artists. Olivia designs logos and websites and Quia is an amazing painter and interior designer. I felt so inadequate. It's common to feel "less than" when you compare yourself to others. That's exactly why you shouldn't do it. It is detrimental to your health and your growth.

We we think about our gifts as it relates to ministry we are often looking for our gifts to benefit the church as in the building and weekly programs. We forget we are supposed to serve the church, as in the people of God. While being a mechanic is not a "ministry gift" in the common use of the word, it is a way to serve the people of God. You might not be in the pulpit on Sunday or wearing a choir robe, but when you are honest and you get someone's vehicle running, trust me you are an answer to prayers. Maybe you're a hairstylist, make-up artist, photographer, or nail technician and it seems like what you do isn't important in comparison to what someone else is doing. First of all, stop with the comparison already. Second, as a speaker and teacher who has had need to have my hair styled, my makeup and nails done, and my picture taken I am thanking God for you. I want to put my best foot forward when I speak or when I have the opportunity to share what I do on television, I want to look my best. I have almost zero skills in that area. If I didn't have access to an amazing make-up artist , stylist and photographer some of you wouldn't even have this book in your hands right now. I would look very busted on the cover of my book. Let's just be honest. You'd ask yourself how can she help me get my life together if she can't even get herself together? I also want how I look on the outside to reflect how amazing I feel on the inside (God lives in me, my inside is on fleek!). We must see our talents as tools that can be used for the good of the Kingdom or for the good of ourselves only. Don't allow the enemy to make you feel as though your gifts aren't worthy or of value because they don't operate in the pulpit. He is such a liar!

There are countless books that delve into the complexity of understanding one's identity and how it impacts us written by people much more qualified than me (ah, the comparison). I however, hope you now know who you are, who God is and that you have a purpose in life. Your true identity is found in God, it is one that is strong, powerful, protected and one that was created for your purpose, and for God.

Power
of
Forgiveness

CHAPTER TWELVE

Power Principle #2

Forgiveness is freedom

Someone has hurt you. Probably more than one person. If you are anything like I was, you probably have a list of people who have hurt you, dogged you or have done you wrong in one way or another. I certainly had a list. Let's start with my biological dad.

My biological dad was not a parent to me. I knew who he was, and he knew me, but we didn't see each other or spend time together. As I mentioned before, not having a dad around was normal for my neighborhood, so I never really had a problem with him. All that changed the moment I had my daughter Micah. Once I became a mother I couldn't imagine not seeing Micah's sweet face everyday. I couldn't handle the idea of not watching her grow up or being a part of her life. Just thinking about not being a central part of her childhood would send my heart plummeting down to my stomach.

I could not put two and two together. He was a grown man, fully capable of providing and caring for a child. Here I was, a teenager with my teenage boyfriend and we had both taken on the responsibilities of being teen parents. Granted, we had no idea what we were doing, but everyday, we got up and made it happen for our little family. No matter how I Rubik's Cubed it, twisted it or turned it, trying to get it to make sense in my head, it never did. My mind literally was unable to tolerate someone "walking away" from their child.

Once I started to see it from the perspective of the mother in me, and not the child in me, I got angry, very angry, the blinders were taken off the bull. All I saw was red. How could he? How could he just leave and never look back? How could you not care how I was doing? What I was doing? Who I was with? What I ate? Where I slept? Everything, and all if it wrapped up in a question mark. Though he'll never get "#1 Dad" mug from me, he will always hold the place of the very first man who broke my heart and disappointed me to no end.

Second place on the list goes to my dad, Danny. He came along and he was great. I love him. He was so much fun and best of all (when I was a kid), he brought me lots of gifts. We would all go on trips together during the summer to Miami and to Disney World. We would go and see my grandmother (his mom) and my aunts in Cocoa Beach. It was good. He was silly and funny. He thought he could dance , still does actually, and I loved it. Like I said, it was great, until it wasn't. Things started to change, first it was slow and sporadic then it was at warp speed and constant. Danny went from being a super lovable, easy going guy who always had a smile to share, to being a mean impulsive alcoholic yelling and arguing with my mother.

Living with an alcoholic you never know what version of them is going to walk in the door. The minute you hear the car pull up, your body goes tense, stiff as a board. Should I stay on the couch watching tv, or should I go to my room to avoid him? I remember one particular night more than the other nights. Danny came home drunk and really mad as usual. He started yelling and cursing about something or other, so I went in the room with my little brother Mario. We were quiet and waiting for the air to clear before we would come out. Well, I overhead him refer to me as a "b!+ch" so I just decided to leave and take my brother with me. It was dark out, but it didn't stop me from walking down the dirt road away from the house and the insanity. I'm not sure where I was going because we were a few miles away from anyone I knew well. When we were a little way down the dirt road, I heard them come outside. I stopped for a minute because I could hear they were still arguing. I looked back towards the house, but it was too dark to make anything out. That's when I heard it.

POP!

A gunshot.

I knew he shot her. I grabbed my brother and ran like there was no tomorrow dragging him right along with me. I ran to the neighbors house down the dirt road, he was standing outside with a few other guys. I recognized one of them, it was my friend Charmaine's dad. I was crying and screaming "He shot my momma, he shot my momma." Someone called the police.

Turns out Danny had only shot into the air. My mother hadn't been shot, she was fine. Didn't matter though, the police were called and he was taken to jail. We moved out for awhile after that incident, but we eventually moved back home. My guess is that he made promises about getting better and changing his ways although I can't know this for sure. Whatever he said to get my mother to come back worked because we were back. Unfortunately it didn't have much impact on his drinking. We were together but that night changed everything. It would never be like it was before.

Sadly, he still drank and came home drunk. When he was around I'd wish that he wasn't. The way I saw it, he chose drinking over us. He chose alcohol over his family. Although my biological father broke my heart and disappointed me, Danny was different. With my biological father there was a mystery about who he was and what he could have been. There was a curiosity and hope of what he may have been had he wanted to be a parent.

With Danny, I knew who he was and he knew me. There was history, memories and a time before the alcohol, before it all went bad. I knew Danny's smile and the way his eyes would light up when he was dancing at a wedding or family gathering. He swear he can dance. There were memories of holidays, birthdays and fun vacations, and the life that we had with him. It was painful to know we would never have that again.

Eventually the promises to do better and be better grew tiring and my mother divorced him. I was relieved we wouldn't have to live in that environment anymore, but I still held on to the hurt, bitterness and resentment I felt for him for a long time. While I no longer harbor any resentment towards him, the truth is I was more hurt by his actions than my biological father.

The list doesn't stop there, it goes on to include my husband and myself along with countless others in my life. You've read our troubled love story so you know how Michael hurt me and the hurtful things I did and said to him. I am not without blame. Not just in my marriage, but in my life. Just as I had a long list of people who hurt me, I am sure I am on more than one list as someone who has hurt others.

I could give you a million excuses about why I did what I did, but the truth is motive has little impact on the pain you feel when someone has hurt you. When we are the victim we tend to believe the other person's motives were heinous, malicious and intentional. When we, however, admit to the pain we cause another person, seldom was it our intent to do so. We give ourselves justification, we compare and contrast the severity of what we did to the severity of what was done to us.

Honestly, it doesn't really matter how, why or what the hurtful act was, when we hold on to that pain it changes us. We remain broken, become bitter and the resentment threatens both old and new relationships. We carry around a heavy burden of all our hurts and the longer we live and experience life with other imperfect people the burden gets heavier and heavier. It is poison to our souls, our lives and our future.

Even though I knew my true identity, it didn't heal the hurt and pain I felt on the inside. I realized if things were ever going to change for me I needed to learn how to forgive others and I needed to forgive myself. We are all children of God, but if we hold on to the bitterness and resentment that has developed over the years we will not be able to live our best life. Forgiveness isn't for the person who has wronged you, it's for you.

It can be difficult and seemingly impossible to forgive. We remember all too well, what was done to us and what we have done to others and to ourselves. The enemy of our soul is happy to remind us should we even attempt to move on with our lives making it all the more difficult. I believe before we can forgive anyone, we must first realize we have been forgiven. It is what has set you free from the wages of your own sins and wrongdoings.

> *"In whom we have redemption through his blood,* **the forgiveness of sins,** *according to the riches of his grace." Ephesians 1:17 KJV*

Let's turn for a moment to how we have been forgiven. The scripture clearly states forgiveness of sins. Which means you are not without blame. You don't need forgiveness if you have lived a perfect life. As a child of God you realize you've been forgiven for the things you've done. You can look at yourself and recognize you aren't a horrible person. You are not a monster, but you may have made some bad decisions.

Some of those decisions you knew were wrong, you may have enjoyed them immensely, and maybe even relished in the fact that you were being such a rebel. You've said or done something which has hurt someone else. Someone has been hurt by your words or your actions. Knowing this about yourself and the fact God still forgives you should inspire you to apply that same level of compassion to others. Don't look at people who have hurt you as if they are monsters or evil set out against you. They are just people, imperfect, broken, and hurt just like you.

Remember, you lived a life of sin before you came to know Christ. The bible tells us the wages of sin is death. The crazy part is that while you were out partying in the USA and giving in to the desires of your flesh, God had already made a way for you through Christ Jesus. Think about it for a moment. While you were still a sinner Jesus had already paid the price for you and you were already forgiven. You just need to accept it. Jesus didn't wait on you to get your life straight to die on the cross. He didn't say "Let's see if she is really sorry first, then I'll lay down my life." He didn't withhold forgiveness for a few months to determine whether or not you would go back to your old ways or make the same mistake again, either. Nope. He made the decision to forgive you before you even knew you needed to be forgiven. Maybe you didn't accept his forgiveness until recently, maybe you are still struggling with the fact that you are forgiven, it doesn't change the truth of God's forgiveness for your sins.

This forgiveness was prepared and delivered on the cross long before you even existed. It is a gift you receive by faith. Sometimes we may feel like we don't have to forgive until someone comes to us admits their wrongs and asks for forgiveness. Our standard, however, is Christ. We as people of faith, believers and followers of Christ have a high standard to follow. Maybe they should ask for forgiveness, but we should, like Christ, give it now and not delay.

Perhaps you are thinking you did more than partying? Maybe you were more than mean and unkind. Re-read the scripture and notice it gives no qualification, justifications nor exceptions to the sins forgiveness applies to. The forgiveness we have been given covers all sins. What you did, who you did it to and the motives behind it matter not. It's not mentioned at all in this scripture. The devil would have you believe that whatever secret, darkness you are thinking about at this very moment is somehow not covered. That is a lie! The horrible thing you did that no one knows about, not even your spouse or your best friend, guess what?

FORGIVEN!

We often do only what comes natural or we think everything should be easy. The reality of it is forgiveness is not easy. It can be hard and extremely painful. We shouldn't let the pain of forgiveness keep us from giving it. Aren't you thankful Jesus didn't let the pain of the cross keep him from forgiving you? I know I am. In order to extend that gift of forgiveness he had to pay a very high price. He paid in blood, he paid with his life so that ALL your sins would be forgiven. Did you earn or deserve this forgiveness? No, not even a little. He did this according to his abundance of grace. He did this because of who HE is. This is the example that is set for us. We forgive because we are forgiven. We forgive even when it hurts and we do this from the abundance of grace that lives in us as children of God.

There are, however, added benefits for you when you forgive. It keeps you free. Not only does forgiveness make you free, it ensures that you stay free from bondage. You aren't perfect and even though you know who you truly are, it will not keep you from future sins.

> *"For if ye forgive men their trespasses, your heavenly, Father will also forgive you: BUT if ye forgive not men their trespasses, neither will your Father forgive your trespasses."*

We have an attitude that forgiveness has to be earned or asked for and whether or not it's granted depends on what is done to us. If it was an accident or a mistake, we are more apt to forgive. If, on the other hand, we feel the act was intentional then we want to withhold our forgiveness, especially if that forgiveness is not begged for. We want to add conditions to forgiveness. We will forgive them, if they ask just right, feel guilty for as long as we deem necessary to show the are really sorry and if they never do it again.

If they should be a repeat offender we maintain the right to rescind the previously given forgiveness as they were clearly not really sorry or repentant because they did it again. If we don't believe the perpetrator is actually sorry and we know based on their character or previous behavior they are most definitely going to do it again, they don't even get the courtesy of a temporary forgiveness.

As I said before, forgiveness is not for the offender, it's really for the one who is the victim in the situation. This is in true "God-form," this is his style. The natural mind would have us to believe forgiveness is for the offender, we believe they need our forgiveness and therefore we have the right to set the rules and steps they need to take to be forgiven. Unfortunately for us, God, as he has done for you, has done the same with everyone else. He has forgiven them. They don't need us to forgive them. Outside of all logic and reason, God's word shows us that we are the ones who need to extend forgiveness. It is for our own benefit that we forgive those who have hurt us.

Not only does forgiveness release us from past hurt, failed expectations, deliberate abuse and misuse it gives us what need to move on. We have to let go of the idea that forgiveness is based on some type of merit system, where we are only required to forgive those who meet the specific requirements. If we want to continue to be forgiven, we must forgive. It may not be easy, but it is plain and simple. Say to yourself, "if I want to be forgiven, I must continue to forgive."

When you forgive someone for what they've done, said, or how they've hurt you, you set yourself free from the bondage of that hurt. You are set free from the bitterness, resentment, and the regret. But, when you refuse to forgive, when you hold on to unforgiveness you are enslaved. You remain a slave to what they did to you, what they said about you, and how they made you feel. You are bound in chains to how wrong they were and what their responsibility was or is to you. Those chains then go on to create more pain in your life, not only from the pain of what they've done, but from being bound to your own wrongdoings. God expects for you to follow in his footsteps and because he has forgiven you, the expectation is that you will forgive others. If you don't forgive others for what they have done to you, God won't forgive you. This may seem harsh or like God is being petty, but it's guidance so you can live your best life. God knows when you forgive others you will be free.

He also knows that forgiveness doesn't only give you freedom, but it gives wings to your prayers. If you have been in church circles for any amount of time then you are probably familiar with the following saying. "Whatever you ask God for believe it and you will receive it." There is definitely some biblical truth to that saying, but it's not exactly as you might think. Mark 11: 24-25 says,

> *"Therefore I say unto you, what things soever you desire, when ye pray, believe that ye receive them, and ye shall have them. And when ye stand praying, forgive, if ye have ought against any: that your Father also which is in heaven may forgive you your trespasses." KJV*

The first part of that verse is most encouraging, right? I don't know about you, but I have a ton of desires. Think for just a moment about the desires you have in your heart right now. What comes to my mind is my desire to see the lives of women changed because they read this book, my desire to speak on stages all over this world. The desires that I have for my calling, the desires I have for financial prosperity and increase, legacy, marriage, impact, my children's success, health and healing, love..I mean depending on the day the list goes on and on.

Whenever I pray about these desires I believe I will receive them, which according to this scripture means I will have them...right? Not so fast, the scripture continues to say that while you are praying for all your little heart's desires, if you have a problem with someone go ahead and forgive them so that you can be forgiven. I guess you could argue they are separate and not intended to be taken together, but I am not so sure about that. I am not saying that if you don't forgive then you will not be blessed or that if you are going through a difficult time it's because you haven't forgiven someone. No not at all. I've been blessed my entire life and I used to be the Queen of Grudges. If holding a grudge was an Olympic sport I would be a gold medalist several times over.

All I'm saying is that it seems to me that there is some connection with getting your prayers answered and your ability to forgive others. Think of it like this, when you travel by plane you have the option to check your bags or carry them on the plane with you. You can get through the airport and board your plane just fine even if you carry your bags with you. If, however, you decide to check your bags and leave your luggage at the curb, your time through the airport is much easier. It completely changes the way you board, reduces your stress and aggravation. I believe this is the point of this juxtaposition of blessings and forgiveness in this particular scripture. You can still get the desires of your heart, however, you'll do so under the chains of your own trespasses, under the weight of your luggage. God wants you to live your best life, one without the weight of unforgiveness.

Can I add one more thing before I move on to the next principle? Forgive and forget. I know there is a very popular saying "I'll forgive, but I will never forget." I think you will find that holding onto memories of pain, even after you have forgiven someone will still carry a certain amount of weight and will ultimately keep you from living a life of freedom.

Going back to the travel analogy, the first time I checked my bags I left them at the curb with the attendant, but I still carried them with me. All I could think about as a I navigated through the airport was my luggage. I thought about whether or not they would put it on the correct airplane and what would happen if they didn't. I thought about the pieces of clothing I'd packed and whether or not I could find replacements for them and how much it would cost me to do so. Even though I had "checked" my baggage I never left it there. I didn't enjoy the freedom of not having to lug the heavy bags with me. The same is true for us with forgiveness. If you forgive, but don't forget you will still continue to carry the baggage of your past.

I want to leave you with a challenge. A choice really. Choose forgiveness. Forgiveness is a choice. You make the decision to forgive. It's not a feeling. Maybe you feel like by forgiving someone before you FEEL like it makes you phony or a fake and that's basically lying, right? Nope. Forgiveness isn't about how you feel, it's about making a decision to let go of the past.

Do you always "feel like" cleaning, or paying bills, or going to work? My guess is, there are several things you do on a regular basis that you may not "feel like" doing, but you do it anyway. Why? Because you realize the choice to do them has some benefit for you be it a clean house, lights on in your home or earning a living. The same is true with forgiveness. There are clear benefits from choosing to forgive others and in choosing to forgive yourself as well. You can choose freedom or you can choose bondage. Embrace this new courageous life of yours and choose forgiveness even if it still hurts.

Power

of

Faith

CHAPTER THIRTEEN

Power Principle #3

"You must put your faith to work."

Faith is this invisible force. You can feel it, but you can't see it. It's like the wind. Depending on the strength of it, it can rustle leaves or destroy entire buildings. You can't see the wind, but we know it exists. We can see its effect on the things around us. We feel it move gently across our skin on a cool spring day. We watch as the trees sway from side to side in a gentle breeze. In horror, we watch as it demolishes homes, towns and buildings when it is most powerful, nothing able to stop it or slow it down. Just as you can look at a tree which has been uprooted and know strong winds ripped it out of place. Strong faith can do the same thing in your life. You should see mountains that are moved in your life and in the lives of others by faith.

When you think about faith what's the first thing that comes to mind? For me, it is a belief that led me to salvation. I understand this as the starting point for most christians, but let's be clear, we cannot stop here. Faith has to take you beyond your salvation. Salvation might be the first time you put your faith to work, but don't let it be the last. Your faith is meant to be active throughout your life. Don't stop at salvation. Salvation is not the final destination, it is the starting point.

Faith to pray.

When it comes to your prayer life, faith acts like a magnetic force. The magnetic force is unseen by the naked eye, just like faith, but it attracts certain materials. The stronger the magnetic force the stronger the pull. Our prayer lives are the same. Faith provides a force that draws us to prayer. The stronger the faith the stronger the pull we have to pray. There is an attraction required though. There has to be something in us, the right stuff in order for us to feel the pull and respond.

Prayer is communication with a God you have never seen with your own eyes. If, however, you go to Him in prayer that is evidence of your faith. You must believe he exists, otherwise you wouldn't even bother praying at all. When we pray we believe someone is listening. You aren't just crying out into open air or only crying into your pillow. No. You believe God is there and he is listening. The stronger that belief the more often you pray understanding you have unhindered access to him. The fact that you have direct access to God, the Creator of all things, should have you geeked out right now.

Sometimes we can feel as though we don't know the right people to get us to where we need to get in life. If only we knew someone with {fill in the blank}, then our life would be so much easier, or we would have more opportunities. The truth is we only need direct access to One. The One. I am. And you have it!!! God is the only one who can provide you with opportunities, healing, restoration, reconciliation, and whatever else you need.

When you look at the success of those around you, maybe your mentors or those who have achieved a level of success in their homes, marriages, businesses or ministries you can only dream of having, remember this: The same God that opened doors for them, can and will open doors for you. You have direct access to that very same God and he loves you just as much as he loves them. God doesn't play favorites.

His love is something you must understand by faith. Then allow it to lead you to prayer. Not just because you know he is there, but because you know he will answer. You aren't simply talking to a God you believe is there, no you are talking to a God you believe is there and will respond to your prayer requests. If you are seeking guidance, deliverance, direction or a blessing, you will get it because God answers prayers. You also must understand God cares. He will not just return any answer, his response be it "yes," "no," "go," or "stay" is for your good because he loves you.

Let your faith motivate you to pray because you understand that God is real, he cares for you and he responds. Your faith leads you to pray because it opens your eyes to the fact that not only does he care for you, but he is more than able to handle all of your cares, all of your burdens, all of your hurts, all of your heart's desires. He is without limit. There isn't anything he is unable to do for you. He will do exactly what he said he would do, he can do all things, NOTHING is impossible for him.

The evidence of faith in your life shows up in your prayer life. If you truly believe God is there, he cares, he responds for your benefit and nothing is impossible, why wouldn't you take ALL your requests to him? He knows EVERYTHING. He is the best strategist for any and every situation. He is LOVE, he is the best advisor for matters of the heart and dealing with relationships. He is a Way Maker, he can make a way where there is no way. What would keep you from seeking him in prayer?...lack of faith in him?

After Toucan passed my faith took a serious hit. I no longer believed God was working things out for my good so I didn't spend much time in prayer. Don't get me wrong I spent plenty of time throwing accusations at him and making declarations, but I no longer had conversations with God motivated by my faith in him. The truth of the matter is, I allowed my situation, my devastating loss to change what I believed. If you looked at my life during that season you would be hard-pressed to find any evidence of faith at all. I didn't have faith for my life, for my marriage or my future.

When your situation has been difficult for a long time or when it seems like nothing is going your way, it can be difficult to keep the faith and pray. Sidenote: this is what makes prayer partners so vital to your walk. When you no longer have the faith to pray they can continue to pray for you. These prayer partners will stand in the gap and lift you up until you can return to your right mind...a mind that trusts in and has faith in the goodness of God.

Faith to wait well.

You may feel the pull to pray, but praying does not always result in an immediate manifestation of your needs. This delay can definitely test your faith. Anytime we pray and believe we will receive it, but we don't see what we prayed for coming to pass in what we feel like is a timely fashion, it can be a problem. If we are not mindful it will give way to doubt, resentment, a complaining spirit and overall negativity. These all are poisonous to your faith, your prayer life and subsequently your courageous lifestyle.

Keep in mind most things don't change overnight. It's not that they can't, but usually it doesn't work that way. Because we know God is capable of a "suddenly" miracle we are all hoping we will get a "suddenly" blessing. Recognizing the power of who God is we know he can change our situation in an instant, he can accelerate our growth with just a word, so it's difficult to accept when we have to wait. We never have time for waiting, we need Jesus to fix it right now. Active faith helps us not only to pray, but it helps us to wait well, to have patience.

When I was praying for my marriage, believing God could and would change my husband (I blamed him for everything) I wanted God to respond like Samantha the witch from the old black and white tv show. With a just a wiggle of her nose and the house would be clean. I wanted God to wiggle his nose and fix my husband. I wanted to go to bed with my life, mind, heart and soul damaged and wake up with rainbows, unicorns and butterflies. Let me say it again. "It don't work like that friend." If you are praying about your depression and mental health, they aren't going to improve overnight. Praying about those kids driving you crazy, the family member who's sick, a bitter resentful spouse, addictions, abuse, health whatever it is when you go to sleep, it's probably going to be that way when you wake up.

I don't want to create this fantasy camp where all situations are fixed overnight. That type of false hope only damages your faith. It takes time. It's a process; one that may include some dedicated work from you. When we are living in our need, living through our lack, or dealing with the daily burden of a dysfunctional relationship it makes it almost impossible to stay the course. Almost.

Your faith will help you to wait. You can pray for years for your marriage and not see a substantial change. The evidence of your faith will be seen in your attitude and your actions while you are waiting for things to improve. When you exercise your faith, it keeps you from walking out on a marriage that can be saved. When you exercise your faith it keeps you from giving up on your hopes and dreams because things don't seem to be changing. Your faith will keep you right where you are, no matter the situation. You will continue believing, trusting and holding on to what you are asking God for. You will stay faithful to God's will and committed to doing things his way while you are waiting. You will continue to pray, attending church and serving God even when things seem to stay the same.

I was a woman praying for my marriage, and for my emotional and mental health. I prayed, I went to church, started serving at church, but nothing seemed to change. I had "friends", lacking in faith themselves, who didn't understand why I continued to stay married. I even had one tell me flat out she would NOT be praying for my marriage, but that I would have the strength and the courage to divorce him. From the outside it didn't look like anything was happening.

My positive and hopeful attitude in the face of a failing marriage and a husband who had learned not to trust my kindness was evidence of my faith. It didn't matter what it looked like or how I felt. My hope was not in my ability to change or in Mike's. It was in the Lord. I knew, by faith, that my greatest days as a wife, mother and as a woman of God were ahead of me and not behind. Because of that faith I could wait well. I knew it was just for a season. I didn't know how long the season would last, but through my faith I was able to wait well until I would see the manifestation of the promises of God concerning my marriage and my mind.

Now consider a woman, without faith, praying for her spouse. What hope does she have if after six months of praying there is little to no improvement? Why should she believe that it will ever get better. If there is not a possibility of improvement, then it is not a season, but the new normal. She is thinking it will ALWAYS be this way. Hopelessness can make an already difficult situation harder to handle. She can't continue to pray for a man that will never change, she can't continue to forgive a man that will always be that way. She can't live the rest of her life in misery waiting on a change that will never come. So she doesn't. IF she has great faith, you would see evidence of it in her behavior and her attitude. When you see a tree that has been uprooted that is evidence of the wind. When you see a woman praying for her marriage and continuing to speak life over what appears to be a dead situation that is evidence of faith.

What if I told you it would take 150 days of prayer for you to be delivered from depression, to save your marriage or to see a loved one come to know Christ? My guess is that you would pray each day for the next 150 days. If you knew how long it was going to take you would continue in faith. It is almost impossible to keep hope alive when you aren't sure how long you'll have to do it for or you can't see the end in sight.

When we know the time frame we are more dedicated. You know it will take about four years in order for you to complete your degree and get a better paying job. You commit to that four years and are dedicated because you know in four years things are going to get better and you have decided that it's worth it. You don't get to year two and wonder how much longer it's going to be. You are diligent from day to day, even though on any given day it doesn't look like you have gotten any closer to the end. You stay committed because there is a commonly known timeframe.

When we don't have a time frame, we are more apt to give up, but faith will keep us working toward an end we are unsure of, but believe in. When we are living in a difficult situation or an uncomfortable situation the days seem long. The years go by so quickly it seems, but each day feels like an eternity. If you are praying for your marriage everyday for a month and nothing changes it's not easy to continue being the wife God called you to be. When that month turns into a year and nothing has changed most of us are ready to throw in the towel. We don't know how much more we can take. We take no change as an answer from God to give up. We apply this "give up" principle to anything that takes longer than we think it should.

Maybe you've been praying about your finances for a year and you're still broke and in debt up to your eyeballs. You are still living paycheck to paycheck and see no end in sight. The lack of change or improvement could lead you to believe God is not going to bless you. Now, you are ready to stop praying. Instead of giving up because you've been praying and haven't seen any changes consider the possibility that you need to go beyond praying and waiting to a place of action.

Faith to act.

Faith will push you beyond praying and waiting. It will cause you to take action. You act because you believe (through faith) things are going to get better even if you are unsure of the timeframe. Even when you don't have all the pieces, use what you have as you pray and wait. God will meet you where you are.

If your marriage is in trouble, have the faith to go to counseling and do the work necessary to improve the conditions and temperature of your home. Maybe you are dealing with debt and you've been praying and waiting on

God. This may be the time for you to get a budget or a second job or time to reduce your spending. You can't sit around praying for better health, waiting and refusing to get active and make changes in your diet.

The word of God tells us that faith without works is dead. You are believing God for improved health when you are working out regularly, changing the way you eat, getting proper rest and medical care if necessary. You want to start a business and you believe it's going to be very successful? While you are praying for growth and opportunity you must put your faith to work by actually starting the business and putting yourself out there.

Are you familiar with the story of the children of Israel coming out of captivity and spending 40 years in the wilderness? God had delivered them from slavery by the power of his might and was leading them to the promised land. On the way, they wavered in their faith. They couldn't stop complaining and be obedient to God, and as a result they did not make it to the land God promised them. They remained in the wilderness. While in the wilderness, however, they didn't have to work for anything. Manna and quail fell from heaven, they didn't have to put their faith to work. They just went outside, collected the food and ate.

At first glance it seems like a pretty good life. No working, no shortage, regular meal times, decent place to live, clothes and shoes. They had all the bare necessities. The only problem is that they never reached the promised land. You can stay in your current situation, good, bad or ugly and God will provide for you in that space. Wouldn't you rather live the best life God has for you though? Isn't that what reading this book is all about? Those that eventually entered the promised land and experienced the long awaited promises of God had to work for it. It wasn't just handed over to them. They had to possess it by force. The same is true in your situation. You can settle for the bare necessities, which requires no work at all or the best that God has to offer which will require more faith and work than you can imagine.

Do you want to be in a marriage where all that you need is provided by God and nothing comes through your spouse? God can keep you and love you in a loveless marriage. But, is that the life you want? If you are willing to work and fight for it you can experience marriage the way God planned. One where you are loved by your husband the way God loves the church and he is respected by you as you submit to him. Do you want a business that requires you to live paycheck to paycheck? God will keep you and provide for you when your business doesn't grow. Or, would you rather experience the increase and financial freedom you long for? The latter, will require actual work. What about your health? It's not that bad. You may not be in the best shape of your life, but you're managing. In order to see your body do what it was created to do the way God created it to work you will have to put in work.

Truth be told, we only work for things we believe we can one day have. When God has promised you something that seems impossible only your faith will inspire and motivate you to work towards it. You must put your faith to work in your prayer life, while you are waiting and when you are working if you want to see the promises of God manifest in your life.

Power
of
Relationships

CHAPTER FOURTEEN

My Relationships

My relationships with other people.

As I mentioned before, my first friends were my cousins. They set the tone for all future relationships. We were loyal to each other, we had disagreements, but they never lasted long and there were never any questions about loyalty. As a result, I was fairly confident as I entered middle and high school. I had friends throughout and even getting pregnant didn't cause me any isolation. As a matter of fact, my friend Estela and her mom threw me a surprise baby shower and invited all my high school friends. That type of love and acceptance had a positive impact on how I saw myself as a person. Because of their love and support I never felt like I was unworthy or less-than anyone else in my group. I wasn't an outcast, I was the same old Taquesha they had grown up with and getting pregnant didn't change that.

Once I had Micah, I had less free-time to hangout with my friends, but the relationships didn't change. Everywhere I went I took Micah with me. We hung out at Catisha's house or walked around with Charmaine. Tawni and I would go to the pool in her apartment. I mean, things changed, but nothing really changed about our friendships. I think that's what made it so easy to deal with being a teen parent.

My mother was not the type to keep Micah unless I was going to school or work, but if I needed a break my friends stepped up to do me a solid. My friend David would keep Micah if I called him and he wasn't the only one I could depend on either. My relationship with Mike meant I was never a single parent. He was there when I needed him helping to shoulder the responsibility of raising Micah. He helped with diapers, clothes, daycare, whatever I needed. By the time Mike and I moved to Tallahassee with our three kids, the friendships that were made there turned out to be friendships that would once again raise the bar for my standards in relationships.

When we moved to Tallahassee I reconnected with my childhood friend Shalander. We used to spend time together when we were in elementary school, but then we just stopped hanging out. I don't know why, but we did. When we were in high school she dated my cousin Toucan and so when I moved to Tallahassee I knew she was living there. I wasn't necessarily looking for her, but I am so glad I found her. I needed a part-time job and she helped me get hired at Chick-fil-a. Her cousin Olivia, also from New Smyrna Beach, was the manager there. Shalander and I grew close quick because we are so much alike. She is freaking hilarious….just like me. She was also always ready to knock somebody out….just like me.

We didn't do anything spectacular we just worked together and went out to eat and shopped. What else was there to do? When I went to her apartment I would take my kids with me, just like it had been in high school with my other friends. She and Olivia were roommates and so I would get to spend time with Olivia too. It took us a little longer to develop a friendship she is quieter than Shalander and I ...calmer too. We celebrated birthdays together and when I had a party for my kids, they came through. It didn't take long for this friendship to turn into family. They would take care of the kids, bought them clothes, shoes and toys for no particular reason.

During the dark days of college, my first signs of depression, they showed up for me. They didn't see my "debbie downer" spirit as a reason to cut me off. They didn't find me draining, but instead came to the dark place with flashlights of hope, encouragement and the occasional threat to kick down my door if I didn't get out of bed.

Many of us will go through something in life that seems like it's too much to bear and we aren't our normal selves. There are times when relationships are tested. After graduation I moved south, but Shalander, Olivia and I remained close. Shalander even moved in with us when we first moved to Charlotte. She didn't like it here (crazy, I know) so she moved back to our hometown. There is definitely distance between us, but not much else. She is and has always been someone I can rely on in my time of need.

After Shalander moved back to New Smyrna Beach, I had a crazy idea to start a publishing company. I called Shalander, Olivia and Quia (another great friend I met while living in Tallahassee) to ask them to start this company with me. They all agreed. I thought they were all insane because I didn't know anything about publishing or running a business. We started working on our first business venture. It was a magazine for girls. We researched and had meetings over the phone. Olivia came to visit once for a meeting we needed to have with a web design firm. I was still working so I couldn't really show her around. It was a very short trip, maybe two or three days. She called a few days after her visit.

> **Olivia**: *What's your address?*
> **Me:** *123 Main Street*
> **Olivia:** *okay*
> **Me:** *Why?*
> **Olivia:** *I'm moving there and I want to try and get a place near you.*
> **Me:** *Yeah right*

Apparently she had been thinking about moving and she liked Charlotte and wanted to continue working on the magazine. That was crazy to me! We weren't making any money and even though the magazine was promising it seemed insane that she would be moving here. She did move here and we actually started working on the magazine less than when we lived a couple states apart. We were too busy hanging out, eating out and shopping like back in the day.

And just like before when things got dark for me she was there. She continued to be there for me through my toughest days, allowing me to sleep on her couch for days at a time whenever I left Mike, which was often. We shared our lives together, planning holiday menus and vacations together behaving more like family than friends.

On my journey to this side of depression, there were other friends along the way. Many of them I may not talk to on a regular basis, but I think about often. Friendships where we have allowed the day-to-day responsibilities of being married, working and raising our kids to keep us from picking up the phone, but when we do it's like no time has passed. Nikiesha, David, Catisha, Chantel and Estela (mi hermana)....I love you ladies (and gentleman) and while we don't talk like we used to I thank God for you.

You can't expect to embrace courage as a lifestyle and take negative people and toxic relationships with you. When you meet obstacles along the way, instead of pitching in to help you over the hump or picking you up when you are too weak to carry on, they will use the obstacle as an opportunity to remind you of the safety and comfort of what you already know. They will give fuel to your negative self-talk instead of putting out the flames. When you question why you thought you could have better, do better or be better, they will echo those questions, or worse remind you of all the reasons you can't do the very thing you have set out to do. You know these people. They are the naysayers. They say "nay" to everything.

I remember when Mike and I where going through a difficult time I had a "friend" who told me she wouldn't be praying for things to change for us, but that she was praying I would get the strength to leave him. Even though, I "hated" Mike at that time, there was this anger that stirred up inside of me, followed by doubt. She, unknowingly, gave fuel to the constant conflict burning within me. Was I too weak to leave? Was I pathetic for staying? If it weren't for friends like Olivia, Shalander and Quia who hated to see me hurt, but stood in the gap praying for me and speaking words of encouragement to me and life over my marriage, I might have given up. My closest relationships to this day are with people who amplify my faith instead of with people who amplify my fears. That is absolutely paramount to living a courageous lifestyle.

As I write this chapter I am reminded about how important relationships are and how blessed I am by the people in my life. My family, my friends and my husband throughout my life have supported me in my darkest hours and celebrated my brightest days with me. Having great relationships reinforces the positive things you believe about yourself. They remind you how awesome you are, they remind you of your talent, calling and purpose, they also hold you accountable in areas where you need to improve.

My relationship with words.

During my childhood I remember my mother encouraging me and giving me advice and instruction. She always talked about the importance of education. "No matter what happens they can never take away your education." We didn't necessarily talk about how I would get educated or where I would go to college but it was just something I always heard her saying. She also often spoke about the importance of respect on a job. She was never going to allow someone to talk to her "any kind of way" on the job. If they didn't respect her or treat her with respect she would leave there just like she came there... looking for a job.

These words had a profound impact on me. From a young age I decided I would go to college no matter what and I would also not allow anyone to talk to me "any kind of way," not on a job and not at school either. As a result of her words I worked hard to get educated and I took no crap on any job. It wasn't often I ran into someone disrespecting me, but I kept that power inside knowing if they decided to get crazy I could and would leave. I wasn't a slave, not to my job or my circumstances.

Unfortunately, she also spoke words of "worry." Can't really remember any specifics, but I just remember always having this feeling she worried a lot. She worried about us, she worried about money about what people thought and how different situations would turn out. They didn't have as big an impact on me because they weren't words spoken to me, but I sometimes carried the weight of them.

With the age difference between my siblings and I there wasn't much arguing. There was arguing and certainly disagreements between cousins or whatever, but there were rules. There were certain things we couldn't say even though no one ever told me what those words were. I somehow knew there was a line that we couldn't cross, especially when fighting with someone you loved.

When I met Mike that changed. He had been raised with a slightly different philosophy. It was an anything-goes-and-all-is-fair-in-love-and-war type of thing. Nothing was off-guard, nothing was off limits during an argument or disagreement. You could say anything, call each other names..whatever. As we started to build our life together we adopted those rules of war for our family as well. We would fight and argue and you could hear things like"

"shut the f*** up,
stop acting like a b****,
kiss my a**,
suck a d**,
you're a f****** punk,
you ain't s*** you ain't got s*** ain't never going to be
s***,
f*** you mother f***** ...".

Yep, the same lips we used to say "I love you" were the very ones we used to tear each other apart. Didn't really matter where we were either, alone, in front of the kids, out in public or wherever the mood would strike us.

Even fears and doubts I shared, during moments of vulnerability could later be used against me in an argument. He said some of my deepest, darkest fears to my face when we argued and I returned his insults with insults of my own echoing his deepest, darkest fears as well.

After the fighting was over and we made up, he seemed to move on, unbothered by the things I said. I, however, was unable to do the same. His words stuck with me for days after we made up. I started to believe he felt trapped and he used the times when we argued as an opportunity to share his true feelings. I felt as though, the nice things he said when we weren't arguing were just the things I wanted to hear, but had no truth to them.

I learned to use my words as a weapon. I even took pride in my ability to verbally assassinate anyone who dared to upset me, disrespect me, or aggravate me in anyway. I was like a ninja. My words were quick and they cut deep. It was my intention to leave my victim stunned and unable to respond.

Unfortunately, I began using my words against myself. I started with negative self-talk, telling myself how pathetic I was to love someone so deeply and so madly that obviously didn't feel the same about me. I wondered how I had become the girl unworthy of love and affection, but was too dumb to realize it until now. I started to tell myself that if people knew me as well as he knew me, they would know how much I sucked too.

As I continued to internalize every negative word my husband said to me or about me it fed and nurtured my depression. Not that he was to blame for my depression, but holding on to those negative words and allowing them to grow and take root in my mind and my heart was a perfect environment for depression to grow and flourish.

After a while I started to say things like, "I hate my life!" I said it all the time, anytime there was the slightest disappointment.."I hate my life!". No cheese for my grilled cheese sandwich, "Seriously?! I hate my life!" I said it without thinking around my husband and our children. "My life sucks!"

I would sometimes find myself meditating on the insults he hurled at me. I started behaving as if the lies were true. I added my own negative lyrics to the defeating song I had on replay in my head. If things didn't go right, if I lost my temper, if I failed at something that was a perfect opportunity for me to replay the negative track again.

My relationships with people were pretty positive, but my relationship with words was toxic. I had become fluent in the language of the enemy. I was speaking lies, death and destruction over myself, my marriage and even people I loved and cared about.

My relationship with myself.
My personal story with self-care goes back only about a year before writing this book. Adding the relationship with myself was one that was actually realized once I had already started writing. I never really gave much thought about my relationship with my body until my own body started turning on me. With all the responsibilities I had from a young age as the result of being a teen mom, my main focus was work. "Relax" was just not something I did and I definitely didn't have time for.

Red Flag #1
I remember when I was working at a Nursing Home in New Smyrna Beach. Mike and I were already married and we had all three kids by then. I had just finished up at the community college and we were only a few weeks from moving

to Tallahassee, where I would attend Florida State University. I went to work as usual. We had a staff meeting before my shift started and I became very hot. It was like a heat wave that no one else was experiencing. After the meeting I went to my floor to report and then it happened.

My heart racing, pounding like an elephant stampede across my chest. I was fighting for air. I could see people talking to me, but I couldn't hear anything over the pounding of my heart. Everything else was silent and had slowed to a snail's pace. Next thing I know I am dropping in slow motion to the floor. I couldn't stop myself, it felt like a dream..or a nightmare. I wondered if I was dying, I felt a muted panic about missing my kids growing up. Everything was dulled by the pounding of my heart. I looked up at the ceiling as people moved frantically around me. I could hear myself saying "I can't breathe, I can't breathe." Someone pushed an oxygen mask on my face. My erratic breathing caused the mask to stick to my face. It felt like someone had placed a plastic bag over my head. My pulse was at about 165 bpm and I was "resting" so they called an ambulance. I was put on the stretcher, rushed down the hallway and taken to the hospital.

By the time we arrived at the hospital, my heart rate was normal and I felt much better. Exhausted, but definitely an improvement. They ran a few tests on me and reported it wasn't a heart attack. The doctor asked if I was stressed about anything. "Nope," was my reply. For the first time in a long time all I would need to do was take care of my family and go to school full-time. I would probably have to pick a part-time job, but that was still an improvement.

Turns out it was an anxiety attack. Feels like a heart attack, but doesn't damage your heart. They sent me home with a heart monitor for a few days and everything turned out okay. You would think the situation would have given me cause to pause and re-evaluate my life and how I was caring for myself. You'd be wrong. I went back to life as I had always known it, working, family and school, never slowing down. I didn't have any issues with my heart or chest until about 13 years later.

Red Flag #2

It was December 22, 2016, the day before my 36th birthday. I was laying in bed napping with my husband when I felt this sharp pain in my chest. It woke me from my sleep. I knew it must be something serious to wake me from my sleep. I sat up and it was difficult for me to breath. I quietly got up so as not to disturb Mike, I slowly got dressed, sans bra, and drove myself to urgent care without saying so much as a word to anyone in the house. The truth is the pain was so severe I was afraid something might be seriously wrong so I wanted to go alone. Urgent care is less than ten minutes from the house, it was a quick trip. On the drive over I kept saying, "I am not having a heart attack the day before my birthday. I am not having a heart attack the day before my birthday."

Once I checked in and told the receptionist my symptoms: "Shortness of breath, sharp pain in my chest, pain down my left arm" they took me to the back room straight away. I lay there on a small bed with wires being connected to my chest as the doctor asked questions.

Her: Where is the pain?
Me: In my chest, mostly the left side

Her: Is there pain anywhere else?

Me: I can't really lift my left arm, it feels weird.

Her: Why didn't you go to the ER?!

Me: I am NOT having a heart attack.

Her: Have you had a heart attack before?

Me: Nope and I'm not having one now either. I said my chest hurts, not my heart. My heart is fine.

Her: Ma'am!

After a few minutes the results were in, I wasn't having a heart attack and I hadn't had one either. The doctor returned with more questions.

Her: Do you have a stressful life?

Me: No, I have a regular life.

Her: Have you been in an accident?

Me: Nope

Her: Did someone hit you in the chest?

Me: (chuckling and crying a little from the pain of chuckling) Yeah right.

Her: Blank stare

Me: No ma'am, no one hit me.

Her: Tell me about your life, what do you do, what about your home life?

Me: I'm a wife and mother of three ages 19, 16, and 13, we have a cat and a dog, my mother lives with us too. I teach high school Spanish at a charter school. I am an entrepreneur trying to get two business ventures off the ground....that's about it.

Her: Okay, so that's stressful.

Me: That's not stressful, that's my regular life. It's been that way forever.

Her: Okay, well... maybe you forgot someone hit you in the chest then?

Me: Lady, didn't I tell you no one hit me?

Her: There are only 2 causes for this: blunt force trauma or stress so you pick one.

Me: uh...

Her: That's what I thought, what do you do to relax?

Me: (Smiling) Relax?...I sleep.

Her: Sleeping is not relaxing.

Me: oh

Her: You need to incorporate relaxation activities into your daily routine.

Me: okay

Her: Do you understand what has happened? Your chest wall is inflamed, that's why it's difficult for you to move and difficult for you to breath. Your stress has manifested in a physical way in your body. The next time it does, it could be with a heart attack. You have to take this seriously.

Me: I will.

I did relax until I was feeling better and then everything went right back to normal.

Red Flag #3

Then in the spring of 2017 I got sick. It wasn't a big deal, it felt like a virus, but didn't behave like one. I had diarrhea accompanied by, painful stomach contractions, feelings of nausea and trembling. After the episode would pass I would be exhausted and need to rest. Then I would be fine. Well, that would happen a day or so at a time for maybe two to three weeks. It was very frustrating because I'd never know when it was going to hit or for how long. This wasn't the first spring, it had been going on for maybe three to four years. This year my primary doctor suggested I see a specialist.

The specialist ran some tests and told me my body was mostly in good shape. He asked me if I was stressed? I gave my default answer to that question, "Nope". He went on to explain he believed I had IBS, or Irritable Bowel Syndrome. It is caused by stress, anxiety and/or depression. You've gotten this far in the book, so you know I was three for three.

Basically IBS means that your digestive system, while not physically damaged, does not behave properly. There are foods that can exacerbate the symptoms and stressful situations can also increase the frequency of an IBS episode. He also said there was no cure for it. This is something I would deal with for the rest of my life and I was only 36. I needed to incorporate stress-reducing activities into my weekly routine as well as add in a few relaxation activities. If I changed my diet, I could limit the foods that were prone to cause episodes and get some relief. He also wanted to prescribe me an antidepressant to help me deal with my anxiety. I refused it. I'll tell you why. I felt like I had never taken self-care seriously. I wanted to try the natural way of taking care of myself first and if that didn't work, I could always call him for the prescription.

After being diagnosed with IBS I had more episodes than I had in the years prior combined. It was all I thought of, it consumed me. I changed my diet as he recommended mostly only eating potatoes and rice with a few vegetables. I loss some weight, but I was still always anxious about whether or not I would have an episode. I tried to relax, do some meditating and what not, but I wasn't really consistent.

I had this trip that came up in March. I was to go to Las Vegas with three other women. I would share a room and probably a bathroom also. That made me more nervous because I only knew one of the women well, Olivia. I was concerned about ruining their trip by monopolizing the bathroom and stinking it up too. I eventually decided to go.

The first morning, I didn't have an episode, but I did have a break down. I was up early feeling the anxiety and worry just coursing through my body. I was overwhelmed by it, so I went into the bathroom and I just crumbled to the floor, tears running down my face. My cries turned to sobs as I began to question my calling. How can my name be Courage and I walk around scared most of the time? How would I inspire women when I could barely motivate and encourage myself? How would I travel the world in my condition? The anxiety was overwhelming, but then I recognized this negative talk as an attack from the enemy. I responded aloud.

"I don't need to be fearless only strong and courageous."

"My transparency, my story will inspire women and the Holy Spirit will encourage me. I will travel the world because this is what I have been called to do."

I realized I had just accepted what the doctor told me as truth. I was wrong though. It wasn't the truth, it was fact, but it wasn't true.

"God's word said I am healed. "

I left the bathroom feeling encouraged and ready for the world. The trip turned out to be amazing. When I returned home I began to pray over my body and over my mind. The problem with my body wasn't medical it was mental. I have control over my thoughts and if my thoughts could make me ill then I believed they could make me well.

My friend Mary Smith (it really is her name :-)) recommended a book for me, "The Miracle Morning". She had read it and thought it was exactly what I needed. She encouraged me to read it quickly so we could do the activities together and hold one another accountable.

She was right, it was exactly what I needed. I started to apply the principles to my day and it was absolutely amazing! After a few days of the Miracle Morning routines I started to get up at 3:30am to have my miracle morning for two hours. My outlook from day to day began to change. After 30 days I was completely hooked and I have stayed with that schedule probably about 80% of the time.

MY RELATIONSHIPS

It was in the miracle morning I realized the power of the relationship with myself. The better I treated myself, the better I felt. I still haven't mastered it and it doesn't come natural, yet, but the impact of taking care of myself is definitely having an positive impact on all the areas of my life.

I used to only think about how relationships with other people influenced us, but then I realized that is not a full picture. The true power of relationships goes beyond your interactions with people, it includes your relationship with words as well as your relationship with yourself.

CHAPTER FIFTEEN

Power Principle #4

"Positive relationships are your life jacket."

When you start living this courageous life you will start doing things you've never done before. Going beyond your comfort zone, going beyond where you believe your resources can take you. It is truly about going after your best life.

Let's say your best life is on the other side of the ocean. There isn't a bridge or an alternate route to take you around it. You must cross it. What are you going to take with you? My guess is you will have to take some supplies with you. Among the supplies will undoubtedly be a life jacket. You aren't sure if you can do it. You think you can, you hope you can....you are being led by your faith, but there is no guarantee your little boat will make it to the other side of the vast, mysterious ocean.

You get in the boat, you row out to the middle of the ocean and you realize the boat won't go any further. You hoped it would, but it just won't go. You sit in the boat wondering why you've come so far only to not make it to the other side. You begin to question a lot of things, including whether or not your best life is even on the other side of the journey. You consider going back to shore, back to a life with which you are familiar even if you were unfulfilled. You feel something prompting you to get out of the boat and walk the rest of the way. Clearly you have lost your mind, because there's no way you can walk on water and you know you can't swim that far so...no. You can't shake it though, your faith is starting to kick in and it's pulling you toward your best life. You stand up as you prepare to walk on water. You didn't realize it before, but you have an audience. There are other people out in the ocean. Most of them are in boats, but not moving, just sitting watching you.

Just as you are starting to feel inadequate and ill-equipped for the journey, you remember your life jacket. You pull it on and secure the straps. You feel better just knowing it's there. You pray, you gather your courage and you step out of the boat, one foot at a time. It's wet, but you don't sink, you slowly pull your remaining leg over the boat's edge to stand on the water. It's overwhelming. As you prepare to take more steps away from the safety of the boat and closer to your destiny you notice the waves are getting rough. They are crashing all around you. There are people around who are watching this unfold. They begin yelling and waving for you to get back in the boat. Some yell insults at you for even trying to do something so crazy. Why are you trying to do what hasn't ever been done before? And if it has, it's been an achievement of someone more qualified, talented or skilled than you. At least that's what you are beginning to think and that's what your captive audience is telling you. They are trying to warn you of the dangers that lie beneath the surface that will destroy your life and make matters worse. They want you to do like they and everyone else is doing and get back in the boat.

Are you believing God for the impossible? Have you heard a call on your life and you want so desperately to answer that call, have you heard a promise from God and you want to see it come to pass in your life? Maybe the impossible in your life is getting out of debt, finishing college, leaving your hometown, starting a business, reconciling a relationship with a loved one, or restoring intimacy to your marriage. I won't lie to you. When you attempt to walk on water it's possible you, like Peter, will begin to sink. Maybe you have already taking a few steps of faith and you have gone too far to return to the boat. Maybe your swimming skills are limited and all you can do is float right now. The thing that will get you through this distraction, this setback, or storm is your life jacket.

Aren't you glad you are wearing it?

What does your life jacket do for you in this scenario? It keeps you afloat. Even when you are tired, you can't swim, or the waves become aggressive the life jacket will help you stay above water when circumstances get difficult. Through my journey I have realized that the life jacket is made of positive relationships with others, a positive relationship with my words and a positive relationship with myself.

The most important relationship in your life is the one between you and God. It's in that relationship you learn your identity, have the strength to forgive, build a faith that works and realize you were created for a purpose. It's not the only relationship though is it? It's your relationship with words, others and yourself that will help keep you afloat when you are ready to give up. When things get difficult your relationships will either help keep you afloat until you can find your strength or they will drag you so far beneath the ocean you can no longer see the light. They also shape you. Relationships can either make you better or make you worse so with that type of influence we have to handle relationships with care. Let's start with the most common, relationships with people.

With other people.

Positive relationships create an amazing support group. These are individuals who will lift you up and encourage you. They may even invest time and resources in helping you to accomplish your goals in life. These are the ones encouraging you to believe God for big things and hold you accountable to your greatness. They are not "yes men" saying "yes" to everything you want to do and giving the "okay" to foolish and self-destructive behavior. They are calling you on your crap and loving you through it all. They want God's best for you even when you aren't sure you deserve it. They cheer you on seeing the best in you even when you are at your worst and lowest moments.

In this journey, this courageous lifestyle, you are going to need people on your team, in your tribe and in your corner. We were never meant to live this life alone. We are made for relationships. Whatever the call on your life, there may be moments where God is isolating you, but the journey requires a team effort. The size of the team doesn't matter, it's the faith of the team that makes all the difference. When you have positive relationships they keep you afloat on this faith walk.

Let's go back to the life jacket. It is definitely functional, but just having it on gives you a little more confidence and puts your mind at ease, right? The same can be said for the confidence boost you get from healthy relationships. Love is released into your life which creates a force of positive energy. It can inspire and motivate you to keep trying and persevere. You know that no matter how it turns out, success or setback, they will be there for you.

There is a distinction I'd like to make. Relationships, unlike the life jacket, are not one-sided. Being in a healthy relationship with someone gives you the opportunity (and obligation) to serve them as well. Being in a good relationship with my husband gives me the opportunity to show him love, to encourage him, serve him and whatever else I can give. If both parties aren't trying and giving, it's not a positive and healthy relationship.

During my depression I had nothing to give my relationships. I didn't love myself so I was unable to show love to anyone else. But, once I began spending time in God's word I was filled with his spirit and his love for me. It was from that place I began to pour love into my marriage, and my children, then to my friends and family.

Ironically, my relationships helped me to overcome depression. This is what I mean by positive relationships. Even though I was unable to give, serve and love them during my dark times they saw past that and believed the best about me. My loved ones were willing and able to see beyond the broken girl I was at the time to the woman of courage I was always destined to be.

Living courageously doesn't have to mean you are starting a business or doing something outrageous, it can simply mean you are going into unchartered territory. Why try to do it alone? Once you get out there you will face an obstacle, a storm, or an enemy. You do not need to live courageously alone. We were meant to do life in relationship with one another. The bible says they will know us by our love for one another. It's not just talking about a feeling, it is referring to love in action. One that works together for a common goal. Maybe the goal is overcoming depression, dealing with addiction, recovering from abuse or betrayal, saving your marriage, or going after your dreams. Don't go it alone.

I know there are many people out there that are like #TeamNoNewFriends and there is a narrative that supposes women, especially women of color, can't work together or be trustworthy. Let me clear something up right now. Women not being supportive is #FAKENEWS and the idea that women of color are even more difficult to work with or get support from is #ALTERNATIVEFACTS. On my journey, there have been men along the way who have encouraged me, prayed for me and supported my work, but without question my tribe is women and the majority of those women are women of color.

When I am in a room of women, we believe in strong marriages, celebrate the successes and achievements of one another, encouraging one another and expecting greatness from everyone in the room. Once healthy and positive relationships become your standard, and you begin to give what you know is vital in healthy relationships, you will be surrounded by like-minded individuals.

Building positive relationships are not limited to your geographical location. Thanks to the advancement in technology and increased access to the world wide web you can find like-minded people and connect with them no matter the distance between you. I know social media gets a bad rap, but some of my greatest supporters have come from connections I've made via social media. Some of you reading this book have found out about it via a social media outlet.

What happens when you already have relationships, but you are realizing they aren't positive or healthy. Maybe some of them are even toxic and abusive, what can you do? The easiest thing to do is simply seek positive relationships. You don't have to cut anyone off or have crucial conversations right away. Start adding more goodness to your life and you will find the courage to have the difficult conversations necessary to improve or even end relationships. Staying in a relationship while working through issues doesn't mean sharing space especially if there is physical abuse. Safety has to be a number one priority in those instances.

Sometimes you have to do things outside your comfort zone as you search for and cultivate new relationships. Going to a networking event, or conference maybe even traveling alone is a great way to find your tribe. I've met women all over who had traveled alone to attend a conference or event because they didn't have anyone like-minded who was willing to join them. You have to put yourself out there. I know it's not easy, especially for my introverts, but truth be told, if you show up to an event alone there is sure to be an extrovert there that will walk right up to you and spark a conversation. It's definitely time to make a change if you are ready to embrace courage as a lifestyle. I don't want you to stop with just your relationships with people though. Remember, your life jacket on this journey is made up of your relationship with the words you speak as well.

Your relationship with words.

There is a relationship between each individual and the words they speak. You are either using your words to create life or to destroy it. We have creative power as we are co-creators with God. He said "let there be light" and light was manifested. Jesus said we could tell a mountain to move and it would do so. We send our words out to do work. We send them to work for us and toward our vision or to stand against us and destroy the vision. I heard a sermon once by Pastor Steven Furtick. He said every time you say something you should follow it with "and that's just the way I like it." It's a great exercise in helping us to see that what we say we create and if we don't like what it's creating then we should stop saying it.

"I'm so broke, I don't have any money" (and that's just the way I like it). See what I mean? God wants you to know you can have what you say. Instead of repeating your current situation and stating the natural state, start speaking what you'd like to see. Get away from the culture of complaining, "I'm broke, my marriage sucks, nobody loves me, I don't have good friends, I'll always be in debt, my kids are horrible, my job stinks." There is power in your words. Instead of allowing our situations to dictate what we will have, we need to tell our situation what is about to manifest in our lives.

It's quite the cycle. The words you speak, you hear, what you hear impacts your thoughts and what you believe. We experience what we believe. This is true not just with your words, but also the words and messages from other sources. What sources are you allowing to speak to you? Are you spending hours watching reality television where no one can be trusted and the relationships are toxic at best? Then you wonder why you don't trust people or have better relationships. Are you watching hours of news coverage? I understand we want to be informed and aware, but we don't need to watch 24 hour- around the clock coverage of all the ways people are evil and horrible to one another. If we want a different and more positive outcome, we have to pay attention to our input. Good stuff in good stuff out. Which also means bad stuff in bad stuff out.

Speaking positively and using our words to create the life we want to live takes time and effort. It is like learning a new language. In order to speak the language fluently you must spend time building a vocabulary base. Once you have a vocabulary base you can begin to put sentences and phrases together. The more time you spend building your vocab and speaking to others who share your new language the better you will become at it.

Don't get me wrong, I will binge watch less than positive shows on Netflix and Hulu and the music I like to dance to rarely has a positive message. However, I am intentional about increasing my vocabulary. I listen to podcasts (Great Girlfriends, Redefining Wealth, Secret to Success, NonProfits are Messy) all week long. I'm also a sermon junkie listening to sermons in the evenings or early mornings as I get ready for my day. (Steven Furtick, Levi Lusko, Mark Watson, Judah Smith,

Christine Caine, Bishop TD Jakes and Bill Winston to name a few.) I listen to audiobooks, I'm reading books mentioned in podcasts (and there are plenty). I am basically in an immersion program for learning to speak life.

When I first learned to speak Spanish I wanted to use it. I wanted to hang out with people who could speak it fluently or even people who were just learning it like me. It didn't matter, I just wanted an opportunity to get in some practice. The same is true with speaking life. It goes back to the importance of positive and healthy relationships. You can have great conversations about your hopes and dreams with people who also have high aspirations. They want an opportunity just like you to practice speaking life.

I taught Spanish for several years in the public school system and learning to speak another language required me to use my newly acquired vocabulary to communicate. I learned to speak it, read it, write it and understand it when it was spoken to me. We can accelerate our learning by studying the language more and trying it out, even if it's still uncomfortable and it doesn't sound natural. Fluency will come with time and practice.

You also have to consider how your words impact others beliefs about you and your situation. When you are constantly speaking negatively about your relationships, financial situation or life choices you can shape the beliefs of others. When my husband and I would have an argument or fight and I would share it with someone who didn't get to see the best parts of him all they knew was what I said, my point of view. Honestly, it's not even the entire point of view is it? I shouldn't have been shocked when a friend said she wasn't going to pray for things to work out. All she heard about him were the negative things, the fights, the arguments and hurtful words. She didn't know our history, or even the good moments we shared. If I did share anything positive he did or said during that time, it was probably overshadowed by some negative overtone. You know what I mean…"Mike bought me flowers today (positive), but only because he was such a jerk to me this week (shadow). What are you left with? Only a guy who is an insincere jerk.

It's one thing to share with a close friend a difficult situation you find yourself in, but how you share it makes all the difference. This is why I strongly recommend sharing it with God first. Tell God all about it. It will be a challenge to change the way you speak about your situation when the people you share it with are jaded by the words you've spoken over the past. "He'll never change." "I'll never be able to get ahead." "I can't afford to go back to school." For sure there are people who are positive individuals who are living courageously and believing God for the impossible in their lives. They will celebrate your decisions to speak life. You can easily see how your relationship with others and with your words are intertwined. The power of relationships is like a three-strand cord, the first being your relationship with other people, the second being your relationship with the words you speak and the third being the relationships with yourself.

Your relationship with yourself.
Who I share my space with and how I speak about my situation has changed drastically over the past five years or so since my journey began. My relationship with myself, however, is a relationship that didn't even begin until after I started writing this book. When you think about your relationship with yourself, what comes to mind? Are you good to you? Do you

treat yourself as well as you treat those around you? Do you get the same quality time with you that you carve out for your friends, family, spouse or dare I say.....your children? For most of us I think the answer is probably the person in our life we treat the worst or we neglect the most is ourselves. Why do you think that is?

If I were going to blame someone, I would blame the person who taught us what it means to be a "good woman" or a "good man". What the heck did they know? How can I be good to you, when I'm not good to me? Somewhere along the way we bought into the idea that being overworked, overwhelmed and exhausted is a sign of true adulthood. Great mothers are strong and never take a day off. Mothers work 365 days a year, 24-hours a day. "Real men" don't take "me" days or mental health days. The best workers have 257-hours of vacation time they will never use. All of these insane examples are not only expected, but seen as a badge of honor. I hear (and have said) in the entrepreneur circle, "I'll sleep when I'm dead." Let me tell you something if you don't sleep, you will be dead. Whatever the reason, it definitely gets a bad rap. Resting and relaxing has a negative and weak connotation. If you are concerned about "self-care" and it interferes with your 20-hour work day, you feel selfish. How dare you take time to care for yourself? But, what would Jesus do (WWJD)?

Jesus, actually believed in self-care. He would get away early in the day and if his day became too tiring he would leave the crowd and take a break. We don't see Jesus as selfish do we?? Nope. Maybe the problem with self-care is a combination of unrealistic expectations and a misunderstanding of what self-care is. Self-care is often portrayed as a spa day, or day of pampering. While those things are among a long list of self-care options, they do not define it. Self-care is about caring for you. Making your mental, emotional, spiritual and physical health a priority.

In order to have a good relationship with yourself you must make self-care a priority. Self-love is impossible without self-care. When you don't take care of yourself you become mentally and physically drained. You must take into consideration health and nutrition. I'm not talking about dieting, simply healthy living. In November of 2017 I took a step in the right direction concerning my own health. I started working with Kirsten Quick, an amazing health coach and personal trainer. Full disclosure, I haven't been extremely cooperative or interested in the personal training aspect, but I have learned a lot. Working with her has taught me to make food choices based on what will fuel my body. It's not about "diet" foods, but power foods and nutrients that will give the body what it needs. Now, I don't always get it right, in fact I mostly get it wrong, but with Kirsten's commitment to helping me love myself better I have made some improvements. I drink more water, I move more and I eat more veggies. It has had a positive impact on my journey, too.

My mind is clear and as a content creator, speaker and teacher, I need a sharp mind. Your mind can be in a constant fog when your body doesn't get proper care. If you are always fighting an illness or fatigue, how can you do what you've been called to do? We need to eat better and drink more water. We have one temple, our body, which houses the holy spirit. You cannot ignore this. While it is a new area for me, an area I haven't mastered, I have accepted and acknowledged that it is an important part of courageous living.

Before my amazing journey of courageous living, I was only pretending to take care of myself. But now, since I have recognized the importance of relationships with other people, with the words I speak, and the relationship with myself-my life has transformed. These three strands have accelerated the rate at which I've grown. I now have the additional fuel and support I need to continue to do things I've never done, and to overcome the things I've dealt with in my life. I absolutely couldn't have overcome depression without the amazing people in my life, without learning to speak life and taking care of myself.

My marriage would not be where where it is now if it weren't for my growth in relationships and I certainly would not have a goal of reaching over 20,000 women through this book. I wouldn't have had the courage to share my story and the intimate details of my struggles with depression and my marriage. It's doubtful I would have made the decision to pursue the call on my life and go into the land where God has called me to go. If it weren't for my life jacket there is no way I would have been able to keep my head above water with some of the challenges and obstacles I dealt with along the way.

You have to focus on your relationship with others, change the way you speak and start taking care of yourself. Remember self-care is one of the most selfless things you can do. The best way you can show love to other people is to show love to yourself. You can't be there for your children and spouse if you don't take care of yourself. If you want to jump out the boat and walk on water you have to improve your relationships.

Power
of
Growth

CHAPTER SIXTEEN

Power Principle #5

Growth is not optional, it's required

    Coming out of depression was just the beginning. My mind was clearer and so was my heart. I knew God wanted more from me, and for me, than just wanting to live. As I continued to go to church and read my bible I realized God wanted me to serve. He had a purpose for my life, work for me to do and I needed to be ready to do it. It started with Bible study. I had used the word of God to get me out of the darkest place I had ever been in my life. Surely it would be able to take me to the next level in my faith and in my life.

I was still attending Elevation church at the time and Pastor Steven's sermons were amazing and so was the worship. The atmosphere was great, but the sermons weren't addressing all the situations I was managing. It was a great start but it wasn't enough. I needed more than a great sermon. If I wanted to accelerate my growth, and I did, I would have to put in more time.

I wanted to grow as a wife. That was my top priority. While I had a handle on my depression, my marriage hadn't actually changed or improved much. My attitude toward my husband and our the marriage itself had change though. I had become more hopeful and optimistic. If God could bring me out from the deep dark abyss and pull me into the light certainly something could be done about the state of my marriage. I started the only way I knew how….by reading. I read countless books and bible studies on how to be a godly wife. I devoured them, finishing some books in the span of one day. I would immediately apply what I learned to my marriage.

To be honest, it didn't seem to help. Even when things looked like they had improved we would get into an argument and it would be like we hadn't made any progress at all. We yelled and cussed each other out. I cried and fought back the familiar thoughts of self doubt and worthlessness. I swallowed the word divorce like vomit, refusing to let it pass my lips. It wasn't easy and it was painful. I asked God why I had to continue to be nice to him, when he sure wasn't trying to meet me halfway.

Mike's demands seemed unrealistic and unreasonable. He wanted me to stop "nagging" and not use such a disrespectful tone. It wasn't what I said it was how I said it. What he called nagging I called adult conversations about areas where we needed some improvements if our marriage was going to last. There was never a good time to have these conversations and regardless of how I adjusted my tone it was always deemed as disrespectful. I believed he thought I would never be enough. I would never be worthy of the love and affection and the respect I felt I deserved as his wife. Why even bother I asked God. He responded in a way that only God can.

God: What about you?

Me: What about me?

God: Are you perfect?

Me: No, but neither is he and at least I'm trying. I'm going to church, I'm praying, I'm reading these books and what is he doing? Nothing. How is that fair? Why do I have to be the one to do ALL the work? Why do I have to be nice to him and he can still talk to me any kind of way?

God: Why did I have to send my son Jesus to die for you? Why did I have to continue to pursue you and show you love when you continued to do things your own way? Why did I forgive you for the things you've done and things you've said even when I knew you would do it again? And do you think you came to where you are on your own? You think you did ALL the work yourself? You think going to church and praying was all on your own doing? You do know that you can only respond to the call, you can't call yourself, don't you?

Me: Why do we have to go there with Jesus? If you bring up the cross then you always win. That doesn't seem fair and why aren't you calling him too? It's not all my fault and he definitely needs some Jesus.

God: No more than you (smile).

Me: Okay, but I am so tired of trying and still being treated badly.

God: It works both ways. You hurt him and he hurts you. You are not innocent in this.

Me: I'm not innocent?

God: Why don't you focus on you and leave Mike to me?

Me: Uh…..okay, I guess.

I started reading the bible like I was trying to get a PhD in Jesus. I decided to give ten percent of my day to God and his Word. I was no longer focusing on saving my marriage, or keeping my head above water. Instead, I focused on my spiritual growth. Everyday the alarm would go off at 4:30 am and I read my bible for two hours. I would take notes, highlight and write in the margins. I would read another half-hour during my lunch break or at the end of the day. I spent the day meditating on what I read that morning. What did the passages reveal about God? What did they reveal about me? How can I apply what I've learned to my life today? I asked those questions each day. I believe there's a saying, "living things grow and growing things change." I was definitely living and growing. I started noticing the changes.

At first, I changed the way I was thinking and that changed the way I saw myself. I no longer believe that how someone treated me determined my value or my identity. If I hadn't started studying my bible, I would never have discovered my true identity. I never would have understood what it means to forgive or what it means to have faith. My relationship with my words changed because of my time in the word of God. It's in the bible I learned the new language. It's why there is even a book called Courageous Living.

It was clear to me that my personal growth was tied to my spiritual growth. I ran across a book I had attempted to read when I first started to work on my marriage. My cousin's wife, Angela, recommended it to me when things were really starting to take a turn for the worst. It was a book by Martha Peace, "The Excellent Wife." I tried to read it before, but I didn't like it. I thought the concepts in the book were absolutely crazy.

As I read through it the first-time I remember thinking "Angela must really be saved if she's living like this." Her husband, my cousin Pete, is a Pastor and I dismissed the principles from the book with the idea that it wasn't for regular, normal wives like me. It was for wives who had Christian husbands or husbands who were in the church. That's the only way I could see them possibly being feasible. Otherwise, it was a no go for me. When I picked it up again for the second time, however, I realized that it wasn't the book, it was me. So many things had shifted inside me, I could tell that I was now ready to accept the insight being shared in the book whereas before I was completely turned off by it.

Reading the book anew I noticed a constant theme and it began to tug at my heart. I realized that for so many years, I held a belief that my husband was to blame. He was the problem and not me. I believed I was the best thing that had ever happen to him (that part is actually true) and that he should be lucky to have me (that's still true too.) My eyes were open and I could now see the full picture. I had contributed a great to deal to the climate of my marriage. I mistreated him, disrespected him and withheld love and affection when it suited me. My love was conditional and he needed to show that he was deserving of it. With thinking like that it's no wonder we had trouble in our marriage. It also explains why he was reluctant to believe the changes he began to see in our home.

As I grew as a woman of faith I became a better wife. I went from scolding him and giving him the stank eye when I came home from church to offering him a meal and joining him on the couch. My growth didn't stop there, the time I spent in the Word lead to growth, or at least a desire for growth in other areas.

I hadn't ever thought about "personal growth" before. Once I saw how spiritual growth was having positive impacts on my emotional health, my marriage and my relationship with my children, I decided to take a "growth" approach to other areas of my life. I hit the ground running with reading, self-help books, motivational books and any sort of affirmations on spirituality, you name it and I bought it, downloaded it or borrowed it from the library. I immersed myself in self-improvement.

Once things were good in my mind, heart and my marriage I took another swing at entrepreneurship. I had a brief encounter with it in 2007, but it never took off. Somewhere around 2013 or 2014 I started blogging. Someone had once told me if I wanted to get paid to speak I would need to start by writing a blog or something so my tribe could find me. I didn't even know what I would write about, but I knew God had a purpose for my life and I was finally ready to pursue it. The blog wasn't as successful as I had hoped, but I continued to grow and make changes, using my talents and trusting in God.

In 2015, I wasn't where I wanted to be, but I was headed somewhere and I was so excited about it. Olivia and I had continued to work together on our side hustles over the years. I was so grateful for her continued commitment and drive not only to my business ventures, but to her own. We supported each other and knew we wouldn't have experienced the growth we had without each other. We thought there might be other women like us, women pursuing their dreams and wishing they had an awesome support group. M.O.S.A.I.C Women Network was born. The name expressed exactly how we felt about entrepreneurship...**M**aking **O**ur **S**ouls **A**live **I**n **C**hrist. We are a community of women committed to pushing each other forward in business and in life.

The commitment to growth on this journey led me to grow in ways I never even imagined possible. It showed me a new way of thinking and I wanted to continue challenging myself to grow in my way of thinking. In an effort to get exposed to other success-minded people and gain knowledge, I began to attend networking events, listening to podcasts and building authentic relationships with people already embracing courage as a lifestyle.

A friend, Alicia, introduced me to a podcast that would ultimately result in the writing of this book. She suggested the podcast, it was my first actually, called The Great Girlfriends. She didn't give me much description, she just told me to listen. I am so glad I did. That podcast introduced me to many phenomenal women. The hosts, Brandice Daniel and Sybil Amuti are funny, inspiring and down to earth. From the first episode I thought to myself, "these could be my friends for real".

I listened to over fifty episodes in the first two months. Believe it or not, the podcast grew my courage. My journey up to this point had led me to a place where I had courage to fight for my life, my mental health and my marriage. I knew God had a plan for me and I was ready to pursue it. The podcast picked me up from that place and challenged the size of my dream. Was my dream big enough? I called it a God-sized dream, but did I really believe it was going to happen? I didn't.

There were days when listening to the podcast made me cry, not because the content was sad, but because it was so amazing that exposed the doubt I had buried. At some level I believed in myself, my ability and the vision God had given me, but deep down I had roots of doubt and fear. Every time I heard an episode on triumph or where their faith prevailed it was confirmation for me that I could accomplish my dreams.

In June of 2017, I walked away from teaching Spanish without a plan B. Two days later I was in New Jersey with

Olivia, Alicia and my friend Jojo to attend a Great Girlfriends' Conference, when my reality hit me like a ton of bricks. I started bawling, I mean really sobbing. I started rambling with my tear-stained face,

> *What was I thinking? I don't belong here. None of my business ventures have been profitable. Why would I quit my job? I am not like y'all, y'all have real skills. I'm out here quitting my job to focus on MOSAIC Women Network and I feel God in this moment pulling me in yet another direction. I can't...I cannot follow God there...how am I going to make money? I have a family....*

My friends looked at me confused. They didn't know my doubts and fears, but they immediately began to encourage me and make me feel better. Once I calmed down, I decided I would make the best of it and deal with my feelings later.

I can honestly say God used the conference to spark growth spurt. It was a conference like I've never experienced before. It confirmed everything I secretly believed about myself. I am anointed, called and gifted for the work God has set before me. I am not waiting on permission to sit at the table, simply an opportunity (thanks Tieko Nejon). When an opportunity reveals itself I will step up and do what I've been called to do and in the event there isn't an opportunity, I'll create one. I met women who had been where I was and were open and transparent about their journey. It turned out I was right on track. Moments of doubt and temporary emotional breakdowns are par for the course when pursuing your best life.

When I returned home from the conference I brought with me a new level of determination, and a few mentors I would continue to learn from over the next year and a commitment to share my story. Because Brandice and Sybil have been willing to share their stories and journeys with me (via podcast) and invited me into a space (the conference) where other amazing women (Tieko Nejon, Patrice Washington, Evelyn Cooke, Squeaky Moore and Phara Joseph just to name a few) were open to share their stories, I was encouraged. I got the extra nudge I needed to keep moving forward. I want to do the same. I hope my transparency, my battles and my victories have inspired you, I pray it gives you the extra nudge you need to embrace courage as a lifestyle.

You are not your mistakes and you are not defined by your past. You are exactly who GOD says you are. The call on your life is not based on your current situation, it is a reflection of the purpose God has for you. Don't ignore this call because, while it is for you it isn't about you. There is someone waiting for you to manifest the greatness inside you. You have exactly what they need. You are someone's answered prayer.

As you embark on this journey you will face uncertainty, doubts and fears. Don't let them stop you, let them fuel you to embrace courage as a lifestyle. Lean into the unknown because you know all you need to know. God is with you. He is for you and he won't fail you!

Embracing Courage
As A Lifestyle

If you've made it this far, it means you are ready to embrace courage as a lifestyle. You know this lifestyle isn't about avoiding the unknown, it's not about being fearless it's about moving forward regardless. Courage is not a one-time requirement, it is a way of life. As you commit to living your BEST life, the life God has for you remember to be strong and courageous because the storms will come, setbacks and disappointments, mistakes and errors of judgement are inevitable because you are human. Victory, however, belongs to you because you belong to God.

A FRIENDLY REMINDER:
You are a child of God, he is for you, and no enemy can stop what God has for you.

Forgiveness is freedom to let go and let God heal your heart and prepare you for those you are called to serve.

Faith must be put to work, let it lead you to pray, help you to wait, and fuel your actions.

Relationships are paramount to your journey. Develop healthy relationships with others, speak life and take care of yourself.

Growth is not optional, it is required if you have any hopes of possessing your promised land.

Embrace courage as a lifestyle don't run from the doubt and uncertainty, do it scared.

Thank you for allowing me to share my journey with you, feel free to share this book with a friend or two!

love ya!

If you'd like to apply the principles you've learned in this book order Power Principles Courageous Living Workbook at www.couragemolina.com for practical steps you can take.

I invite the ladies to join a courageous group of women dedicated to this lifestyle in the Facebook group Courageous Living Community.

I'd love to hear how this book has impacted you send your thoughts to powerprinciples@couragemolina.com

Acknowledgements

If you didn't like this book, here are the people
you can blame. (Hehehe)

I don't even know where to begin. I am so unbelievably blessed.
God has used hundreds of people over the course of my life to
get me to where I am today.

Michael, I love you with all that I am and respect you more
than words can say. You have been my A1 since day one. No
matter what we've been through I ALWAYS knew I could call
on you and you would be there. Your commitment to our
marriage and our family has encouraged me over the years and
I thank God for you. #lookinglikeaEntree #bae #heeeey
#MypersonalHuck #Lovestory

Micah, Mike & Caira...I love y'all. I am humbled that God
would entrust you to my care. Thanks for being my motivation
to do better, be better, #GETBetter. I am sorry for the dark
days when I wasn't there, I couldn't be there, but I am here

now. When the road gets rough, when you go through storms KNOW that I am standing in the gap, praying for you lifting you up. #Knocksomebodyoutforyoutoo #playwithit #lovemykids

My BFFs: Miley Jackson, Kaleb G., & Paige Henderson...Y'all might be young BUT our friendship means more than you know. Y'all remind me how dope I am and make me feel like I can do anything. I love y'all!

Thank you to my momma, **Joyce Dempsey,** "JJJ", "Junie", and "Danny's Wife" #LOL you gave me life and you cared for me, encouraged me and prayed for me. I LOVE YOU! Thank you for helping me to see the power that God has given me to change the atmosphere of my home and my marriage! I LOVE YOU!! Thank you again!

Thank you **Gladys & Pop Molina** for accepting me into your family back in 1996 and for loving me and my kids without question or hesitation!

Thank you **Natasha Molina** for all the times you listened to me vent about your brother without judgment, but with plenty of understanding and encouragement. I love you! #themotherofyourchildren

Thank you to my sister **Treshawndra Capers** for your support, encouragement and for holding me accountable to my greatness!

Thank you to my brother **Marquis Hunt**, whose reputation and fighting skills kept me from getting in even more trouble than I did!

Thank you **Amario Dempsey,** my brother, blood is thicker than mud, thank you for supporting me and cheering me on! Thank you for telling your kids how dope their Auntie is and for creating a love in them for me that makes no sense!! LOVE YOU! #YesIwillFightYou #IwillFightABOUTyouToo

Thank you **Anterrius** for a shoulder to cry on a place to vent and for thinking failure for me is just absurd!

Thank you **Auntie Hazel, "Baully"**, for raising two of my FAVORITE people in the world. Thank you for teaching me how to braid, for supporting me and loving me. I LOVE YOU!

Thank you **Shalander Charles** for being a great friend to me even though I'm a close talker, with man hands who could drop you like a sack of dirt!

Olivia Heyward, this book definitely wouldn't exist without you. You planted the seed years ago that I needed to tell my story, but I just wasn't ready. You believed in me and supported me in EVERY single business idea and website design I have ever had. You have refused pink slips and never let me quit. Thank you, thank you, thank you. Thank you for loving my kids and for covering my marriage in prayer even when I was unwilling to do so.

ACKNOWLEDGEMENTS

Thank you, **Brandice Daniel** and **Sybil Clark-Amuti** for coming alongside Olivia and watering this seed until I was ready to share a story I believe will save lives, restore families and light a fire to someone's heart and soul.

Thank you **Ms. Ramona Moore Big-Eagle** always reminding me of WHO called me!

Nancy Stittgen thank you for refusing to give me an out when I doubted the anointing on my life!

Robbi Liebert, sister, prayer partner and dance mentor who gave me a chance to do what I love (DANCE) and share that love with others.

Thank you **Awilda Sanchez**, always ready to dance, walk, pick me up, cook me a meal or wash my dishes when I forget (or refuse) to take care of myself. You are my sister and I am so grateful for our relationship.

Thank you **Philip Engle** for "seeing" me and my kids when I sometimes felt overlooked, and reminding me that not only did you see, me but that God saw me too!

Thank you **Nikki Simms** for your infectious faith always challenging me to take God at his word and for your friendship and constant support!

Thank you to **Lauren Mello** for being a sounding board and a safe place to share my ugly parts, my greatest hopes, and my biggest dreams!

Thank you **Stephanie Jeffreys** for showing up, opening doors and not taking any crap or excuses from me!

Thank you **Alicia Moss** for inviting me into your circle and building an authentic relationship with me before I even realized what I really brought to the table. Thank you for making me look like "MONEY" in all my photos! #LOL

Thank you **Patrice Washington** for treating me like a person and not a fan, thank you for answering the call on your life and for mentoring me (via podcast) through this process.

Thank you **Tieko Nejon** for not allowing me to shrink and for setting a standard of excellence that inspired me to be my BEST self and not apologize for my greatness.

Thank you **Pastor Steven Furtick** for preaching with everything in you, for speaking life EVERY WEEK with EVERY SERMON. God, through you, saved my life and my marriage, for that I am grateful. Thank you!

Last, but not least...

Toucan, my heart breaks all over again as I type these words. I can't believe you aren't here to witness what your love, encouragement, and aggravation (smile) has inspired. You believed in me. I LOVE you! I knew my life would never be the same. I miss you and I am a better woman because you lived. What a God we serve that he could even use my greatest, deepest wound and make something beautiful from it! #GlorytoGod #UntilWeMeetAgain

ACKNOWLEDGEMENTS

This could go on for another 10-15 pages. So let me just say this. Thank you to EVERYONE who has loved me, prayed for me, cared for me and fought for me even when I couldn't do it for myself. I am eternally grateful!! Love ya!